Marie Antoinette and the Decline of French Monarchy

Marie Antoinette and the Decline of French Monarchy

Nancy Lotz
Carlene Phillips

MORGAN REYNOLDS
Publishing, Inc.

620 South Elm Street, Suite 223
Greensboro, North Carolina 27406
http://www.morganreynolds.com

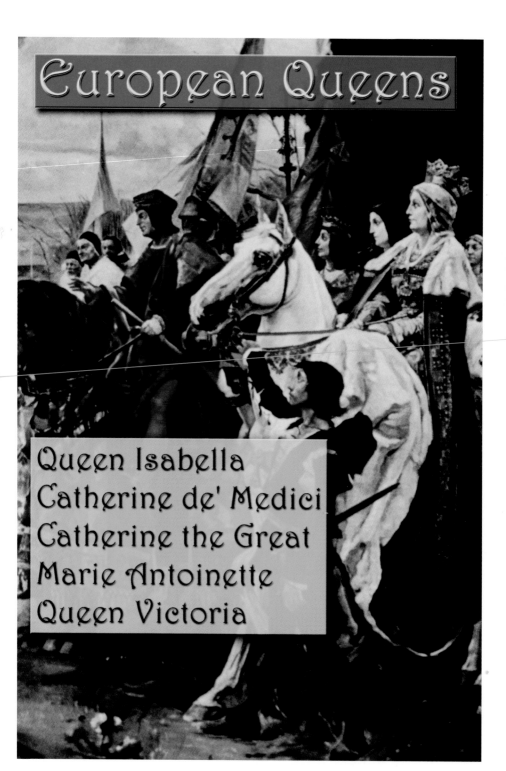

European Queens

Queen Isabella
Catherine de' Medici
Catherine the Great
Marie Antoinette
Queen Victoria

MARIE ANTOINETTE AND THE DECLINE OF FRENCH MONARCHY

Copyright © 2005 by Nancy Lotz and Carlene Phillips

Library of Congress Cataloging-in-Publication Data
   Lotz, Nancy, 1945-
   Marie Antoinette and the decline of French monarchy / Nancy Lotz and Carlene
Phillips.— 1st ed.
   p. cm. — (European queens)
       Includes bibliographical references and index.
   ISBN 1-931798-28-1 (library binding)
1. Marie Antoinette, Queen, consort of Louis XVI, King of France,
1755-1793—Juvenile literature. 2. Queens—France—Biography—Juvenile
literature. 3. France—History—Revolution, 1789-1799—Juvenile literature.
I. Phillips, Carlene, 1938- II. Title. III. Series.
       DC137.1.L68 2004
       944'.035'092—dc22

                              2004014717

Printed in the United States of America
First Edition

To Lilas Lotz and Bob Phillips
for their unwavering love and support

Contents

An Archduchess is Born

On November 2, 1755, the court at Hofburg Palace in Vienna, Austria waited all day to hear the news from the bedchamber of the empress of Austria. Empress Maria Theresa was about to give birth to her fifteenth child. Ever mindful of the responsibilities of government, the empress had spent the day reading political papers and signing official documents. She had even summoned the royal dentist to pull a tooth that had long been bothering her. Meanwhile, her husband, Francis of Lorraine, prayed in the palace chapel. Childbirth, even for empresses and queens, was often complicated and frequently fatal in the eighteenth century. Then, finally, the announcement was made: the empress had delivered her last daughter. Like the previous seven girls, the newborn was given her mother's name,

Opposite: Marie Antoinette *(Château de Versailles)*

Marie Antoinette's mother, Empress Maria Theresa of Austria.

Maria, then the middle names Antonia Josepha Joanna.

The baby's birth was hailed throughout the country; all of Vienna feasted. The festivities were not as grand as they would have been if the baby had been a boy, but there was still much to celebrate. If Maria Antonia, or Antoine as she was called at home, survived childhood, she could grow up to be married to a European prince and, thus, advance

Austria's power and prestige throughout Europe.

In the days following Antoine's birth the empress rarely went to the nursery. The affairs of state were always uppermost in her mind, and the children were left to the care of wet nurses, servants, and governesses. This was the same way Maria Theresa had been brought up. She sent the royal physician to see the children every morning, and the doctor knew more of what happened in the children's lives than Maria Theresa did, even though her office was close by. When Maria Antonia was no more than a few days old, the doctor told the empress that it would be a good idea to relax a little and enjoy her growing family. But she would not hear of it. "My subjects are my first children," she answered. "My first care must be for them; the others must come after."

Maria Theresa's family always put ambition and the affairs of state first. She was the eldest daughter of the Holy Roman Emperor Charles VI, whose empire included Austria, Hungary, parts of Italy and Germany, and the Austrian Netherlands. His family, the Hapsburgs, had been ruling some part of Europe for over four hundred years. In 1711, Charles VI found himself the sole remaining male of the Hapsburg line. At this time, an old law was still in effect that prohibited a woman from inheriting her father's throne. Concerned that he might never have a son, Charles issued a decree, the Pragmatic Sanction, that altered the law of succession in the Hapsburg family so women could inherit the Hapsburg lands. After issuing the sanction, Charles made agreements with some European leaders to honor the succession of his daughter Maria Theresa.

During the last several years of Charles's reign, two wars had left the monarchy financially and militarily weakened. Upon her father's death in 1740, Maria inherited the Hapsburg lands at the age of twenty-three. Charles had fought for her right to inherit, but had neglected to train his oldest daughter about the workings of government. Without money, a strong army, or knowledge of state affairs, Maria Theresa knew she had to rely on her judgment and strength of character.

Her first challenge came from Prussia. Frederick II, King of Prussia, with the secret support of Austria's longtime enemy, France, attempted to take advantage of the transition and invaded Silesia, an Austrian territory. Frederick was a brilliant and ruthless military leader, and this invasion set off a series of conflicts that lasted from 1740 to 1748 and are known collectively as the War of Austrian Succession.

Although Maria Theresa was faced with the prospect of having her kingdom fragmented by a coalition of neighboring forces led by Prussia, the young sovereign seemed undaunted. "Gentlemen, why such gloomy faces?" she asked her advisors. She simply refused to consider the possibility that her inheritance would be stolen from her. In the end, she was forced to cede most of Silesia to Prussia, but she exhibited great integrity and intelligence throughout the long struggle.

Determined to stand up to Prussia, the empress set out to strengthen her state. She established a more positive and efficient diplomatic corp, doubled the number of troops in the army, and reorganized the tax structure to ensure financial support for both the government and the military. Her courage and spirit inspired her soldiers to fight for their country and their empress. It was said at court that Maria Theresa often mused that if she were not with child year after year, she would ride into battle at the head of her army.

Maria Theresa instituted other domestic reforms to improve the lives of her subjects. Her love for her people was genuine; their well-being was never far from her thoughts, and they returned this affection. An enlightened monarch, she distributed power among several administrative units within her empire and appointed commissioners who were directly accountable to her to lead the departments. She instituted economic reforms that both benefited poor peasants and promoted the growth of cities and towns. She encouraged the building of schools and set in place other mechanisms that opened up avenues for upward mobility. Maria Theresa was a powerful leader, much admired and respected by the people of Europe.

By contrast, Maria's husband, Francis, was a mild-mannered, reticent, man. He was from the French province of Lorraine and, because Austria and France had been enemies for centuries, had been forced to renounce his inheritance as the duc de Lorraine before marrying into the Hapsburg dynasty. If he had not done so, Lorraine would have become another Hapsburg holding. It had not mattered much to Francis; he was not a political man. Even after the empress bestowed upon him the title of Holy Roman Emperor, after her own father's death, Francis was not interested in wielding power. He had abandoned his homeland in France simply to marry Archduchess Maria Theresa.

Marie Antoinette's father, Francis of Lorraine. *(Kunsthistoriches Museum, Vienna)*

Once, Francis was overheard goodnaturedly telling a group of courtiers who had insisted upon showing him special honor: "Don't mind me, I am only a husband; the queen and her children are the court." Francis much preferred private life to public life. He deeply loved his wife and children, and his few forays into politics were intended to enrich his family life. He managed to have most of the rigid etiquette of the Austrian Court abolished. Official state affairs were still carried out with magnificence and pomp, but non-ceremonial events became more relaxed and informal, much more so than those found in other courts of Europe, especially at the royal palace of Versailles in France.

Though she was the daughter of one of the most powerful rulers in Europe, Maria Theresa's youngest daughter, Antoine, had in many ways a normal—if extraordinarily privileged—childhood. She was the fifteenth of sixteenth children, which meant she was, inevitably, a little bit spoiled. As her father's favorite daughter, it was left to her mother to provide whatever discipline there was in Antoine's life. Where Francis was tender and doting, spoiling her at every turn, the empress was stern and domineering. Little Antoine, who did not see her mother often, reportedly feared her. She knew, as did each of the children, that her mother would make the final decisions about her future. The year after Antoine was born, her mother declared of her daughters, "They are born to obey and must learn to do so in good time."

Maria Theresa planned to use her daughters to cement Austria's alliances with other European countries. In 1756, France and Austria, two nations that had been enemies since the fifteenth century, signed a treaty in Versailles, a town outside the capital city of Paris. The two nations agreed to join together against Prussia. It was understood that a marriage would be necessary to cement the new bond. The only question was which of Austria's seven daugh-

Laxenburg, the imperial family's country palace.

ters would go to Paris. Several years would pass before that question would be answered.

As Antoine matured, it became obvious that she resembled her father more than her mother. Her elongated face, lips like a perfectly tied bow, and large, widely spaced eyes came from her father and attested to her French ancestry. The color of her eyes, though, was her mother's—royal blue, the color of the sky. She also inherited the prominent Hapsburg lower lip that characterized the powerful family.

The stately Hofburg Palace, where the family spent summer months, was in the center of Vienna. Schonbrunn, a magnificent dwelling in a country setting, was where the family took up residence in the warmer months. During summers, each of the children had his or her own suite of five rooms, including an audience room and a salon. Everyone at Schonbrunn, women as well as men, went riding and hunting. During occasional winter visits to Antoine's favorite palace, the family had sledding parties by torchlight. A

This portrait of the imperial family at home was painted by one of Antoine's sisters, Marie Christine, who is portrayed in the pink dress. Antoine stands between her sister and her mother, holding a doll. *(Kunsthistoriches Museum, Vienna)*

theater, an orangerie, and a menagerie—complete with a camel, a rhinoceros, and a puma—made the palace a veritable fantasy retreat for the children.

There was yet another palace. Laxenburg, the smallest of the three, was set at the edge of the woods and it was the farthest removed from the ongoing state of affairs in Vienna. Here the children were denied nothing, and so attentive were the servants to their every whim that fresh snow was brought down from the mountains so that they could go sledding all winter long.

The theater at Laxenburg was the family's favorite. Its intimate proportions allowed the children to indulge their love of music and their parents to follow their progress. To the imperial family and the Austrian nobility, music was as natural and pleasurable a part of life as was the air around them. The empress insisted that each child learn an instrument. She listened to them play with all the pride of a loving mother. Antoine learned the harp, an instrument she continued to play as an adult.

Little Antoine had a greater talent for dancing than for

This painting, which later belonged to Marie Antoinette when she lived in France, depicts a dance that Antoine and her siblings performed at the wedding of their brother, Archduke Joseph, in 1765. Antoine and Ferdinand played shepherd and shepherdess and Max played Cupid. *(Kunsthistoriches Museum, Vienna)*

playing an instrument. Her figure was naturally petite and graceful. Formal ballet lessons gave her a distinct carriage—head up, shoulders back. This poised and upright posture became her most memorable feature. In contrast to her successes in the arts, the young archduchess was a poor student. She cared little for academic studies and did not have a natural affinity for learning. Her tutor eventually gave up trying to teach her and often did her homework for her in order to avoid the wrath of the empress. As a result, the little girl could barely write her own name.

As the youngest of seven daughters, Antoine was often neglected in favor of her older sisters. Maria Theresa was intent on grooming them—Marie Christine, in particular— for marriage. Antoine and her sister Marie Caroline (called Charlotte by the family) were jealous of the attention their mother lavished on Marie Christine. The two younger girls were often left to their own devices. They developed a close bond in the many hours spent playing happily together.

When Antoine was ten years old, her carefree world was shattered. In August of 1765, her parents were leaving for Innsbruck to attend the marriage of their son, Leopold, to the Infanta of Spain, the daughter of the Spanish monarch. The entourage was assembled and excitement filled the air. The empress was settled in her carriage ready to begin the trip when the emperor, already on his horse, dismounted without a word to anyone and searched for his young daughter among the throng. "Where is my Toinette?" he called out, "I want to give her a last kiss."

The child ran to her father, jumping into his arms, wiping

Maria Theresa in mourning, surrounded by her four sons. *(Schloss Schonbrunn)*

away the tears that were trickling down her cheeks because she was being left behind. Her older sisters were to take part in the wedding festivities, and she had wanted to accompany them, but the empress had refused to let her go to faraway Innsbruck. It seemed that her father was also fighting back tears, his cheeks were moist as he held her to say farewell. As he got back on his horse and started to ride away he turned toward one of his gentlemen. "God knows how much I longed to kiss that child," he said, and then rode on.

One week later, without any warning, the emperor suffered a stroke and died in Innsbruck. The family plunged into deep sadness. Toinette, as her father called her, was inconsolable. Maria Theresa, unapproachable in her own despair, did not think that she would ever recover from the tragedy of her husband's death. For the rest of her life she wore mourning black. The stoic empress was unable to share her grief with anyone, including her children.

Even as she mourned deeply, the empress did not abandon Austria. She managed the affairs of state with her usual commitment and intelligence. One by one, her children were married off for political gain. They had all known from their earliest years that their destinies were intertwined with the state. Their wishes were not important. The girls, especially, knew not to question their mother's choices.

The eldest of the seven daughters was handicapped, and it was decided she would stay at home. After Francis's death, Marie Christine, their mother's favorite, was allowed to marry a lesser noble in order to be able to remain in Austria. Josepha was supposed to marry the heir to the throne of Naples, but contracted smallpox and died. Another sister, Elizabeth, survived the dread disease but was so scarred, she was no longer marriageable. Charlotte, Antoine's next older sister and best friend, was sent off to Naples in Josepha's stead. Suddenly, of all her daughters, Maria Theresa had only young Antoine at home. The youngest, and in many ways the least-regarded child, would have to strengthen Austria's ties to France. As she approached her thirteenth birthday, young Antoine's future became her mother's obsession.

2

Preparing for Marriage

The 1756 Treaty of Versailles had united France and Austria in an alliance against Prussia. The countries of Europe often shifted loyalties as they jockeyed for military and diplomatic advantage. France had supported Prussia when Frederick II had attacked Austria in 1740. But at the end of that series of conflicts, Prussia aligned itself with England. France and England were bitter rivals; suddenly France had to look elsewhere for an alliance or risk being left friendless in the dangerous world of European power politics.

During most of Maria Theresa's reign, Frederick II's Prussia was the most dynamic and dangerous country in Europe. The empress held a long-standing hatred against Frederick. She never forgave him for taking advantage of the internal conflict created by her succession to steal

Silesia away from Austria. Although France and Austria were longtime enemies, Maria Theresa did not let tradition stop her from formalizing an arrangement against their new common enemy.

Even with Maria Theresa's willingness, the long history of animosity between France and Austria was not easily forgotten, and their alliance was tenuous at best. The Austrians admired the style and language of France but believed the French were frivolous, incapable of loyalty, and full of jealousy and intrigue. The French disdained any traditions that were not their own and remained suspicious that Austria wanted to control France for its own best interests.

A daughter of Austria and a son of France joined together in marriage could help to improve the fragile relationship. Fortunately, the timing for such a marriage was favorable. Maria Theresa's daughter, Antoine was only a few months younger than the Dauphin Louis Auguste, heir to the throne of France.

At this time, King Louis XV ruled France. Louis Auguste was his second grandson, but since the boy's father and older brother had both died, Louis Auguste was next in line to inherit the throne. Both Louis Auguste and his grandfather, the king, were members of the Bourbon family. The Hapsburgs had been in power for more than four centuries, but the first Bourbon king, Henry IV, had only inherited the throne less than two centuries earlier, in 1589, after a long and bitter conflict. Louis XV was only the fourth Bourbon to rule France.

The rulers of Austria and the rulers of France had

traditionally followed different philosophies of governing. The French people were taxed heavily to support foreign wars and a luxurious lifestyle for the nobility and aristocrats at home. The poor were rarely, if ever, granted economic reforms to alleviate their burden. In contrast, Austria was generally ruled more benevolently, with a certain degree of compassion and concern for justice. The monarchs of France were famous for their excesses, and were often in conflict with the powerful nobility. Despite these differences, Maria Theresa had made up her mind to pursue France, and young Antoine had a role to play in the strategy.

Negotiations for the marriage began in 1768, and in the fall of that year, Antoine became the sole focus of her mother's attentions. Maria Theresa was angered to discover that her youngest daughter's education had been neglected. She immediately set about shaping the girl into a worthy emissary of Austria.

At thirteen, Antoine was put through a transformation that was supposed to turn her from the giddy and coquettish youngest daughter who romped in the royal playgrounds with her brothers and sisters to a dutiful bride who would one day be a queen. Already known in European royal circles for her beauty, the young archduchess had only a few physical flaws. But even a few were unacceptable. Maria Theresa knew that the future mistress of Versailles, the French royal palace, must be as near to perfection as one could be—a young woman to be envied and imitated.

A Parisian hairdresser was engaged to create a new hairstyle to conceal Antoine's thin hair. Her fair-colored hair

Antoine at age thirteen. *(Schloss Schonbrunn)*

was pulled back from her forehead and raised high, softening her face while highlighting her exquisite, porcelain-like complexion, the color of a pale pink rose. Her teeth were deemed imperfect, so a dentist was summoned from France. Maria Theresa hired the renowned French dancing instructor Noverre to work on how she moved. He taught her how to glide so that her robes would not trail on the floor, a technique fashionable at Versailles. He also taught her the dances popular at the lavish French Court. He practiced with her until her movements seemed effortless.

The marriage negotiations took several years to complete. The French were not at first in favor of an Austrian match. Actually, King Louis XV himself was not opposed, but most of the French nobility were suspicious of Austria's true intentions. They knew Maria Theresa was a smart and accomplished ruler and wondered what she really hoped to gain. For her part, Maria Theresa was nervous about Antoine's ability to represent Austrian interests in France. A foreign queen needed to win the respect and admiration of her new subjects while remaining secretly aligned to her homeland. She doubted that Antoine had the mind for such intrigue. Maria Theresa wrote several letters to Louis XV explaining that her youngest daughter was immature for her age, and hoping he would be patient with her.

Even after the broad outline of an agreement was reached, there were months of discussion over the proper order of the signatures on the final document. This impasse was finally resolved when it was suggested they have two contracts. That way each country could sign their copy first. Maria Theresa then instructed her ambassador at Versailles, Count Mercy d'Argenteau, to find the bride a suitable dress and other clothes. Fine, expensive outfits had never been a priority at the Austrian court, but now Antoine's had to be made in Paris of the best material and the finest workmanship. Her trousseau would have dresses in fabrics and colors suitable for each season, and there would be outfits for every special occasion. Dressmakers from all over France competed for the young girl's approval. They sent samples to Vienna on dolls resembling the archduchess. She was delighted by these small imitations of herself garbed in gowns, robes, shoes, and accessories. She favored the pale yel-

Count Mercy D'Argenteau, the Austrian ambasador to Versailles.

lows, greens, blues, pinks, and silvers that she knew flattered her own doll-like face and figure.

Versailles was the most refined court in Europe. Once married, she would be a part of its grandeur, dressed in these dazzling gowns. She was happy that petticoats for everyday wear were becoming the rage and that she would not have to endure too often the cumbersome hoop skirt that spread out several feet on either side of the waistline.

Not satisfied with just a physical makeover, the empress had a bed for her daughter brought into her own bedroom so that she could tutor her in the ways of royalty. Maria Theresa was sending her daughter to a world very different from the one in which she had grown up. Her own court was informal and had the feeling of a big, extended family. The

French court, on the other hand, was noted for its strict etiquette at all times. It was also known for its immorality, intrigue, and corruption. In explaining these differences, the empress reminded her daughter that she would have to adapt herself to the French court and advised her not to express dissatisfaction or unhappiness with the French ways. At the same time, Maria Theresa exhorted her daughter to always be proud of her Austrian heritage. It was a complex set of instructions for young Antoine, to embrace French ways but to always remember that she was Austrian.

To further enforce upon her daughter a sense of duty and proper royal conduct, the empress showed her a letter written by Antoine's father to be read by his children when they were preparing to leave their homeland. In it he admonished any sovereign who lived in luxury while his subjects struggled in poverty. While Francis Stephen certainly meant well, and the letter expressed the high-mindedness of an enlightened ruler, the letter seemed to contradict Maria Theresa's explicit instructions that Antoine should try to fit in at her new home.

The most difficult challenge was Antoine's insufficient education. Determined to have Antoine's education be equal to her new husband's, Maria Theresa set her daughter on a rigorous course of study. Her spelling was terrible and her handwriting resembled a child's. Even under the watchful eye of a tutor, her strokes improved little, but her signature was at least legible enough to be understood. As a child she had learned French, but she spoke it poorly. Even her native German was flawed. The empress decided that perfecting her daughter's French was most important. She sent for the Abbé Mathurin Vermond to come to Vienna from Paris. He taught the archduchess French history and discussed French literature with her. She enjoyed the history lessons but found the task of perfecting her French daunting. Vermond offered Antoine and her mother a ray of hope: "As for her French," he said, "it will perfect itself as soon as she gets away from hearing German and, what is even worse, the bad French spoken by the Vienna court."

Antoine met other challenges more successfully. She was quick to learn the etiquette that defined royalty and acquired a presence and grace unusual for one so young. Antoine was pleased that her mother gave a ball in her honor in the fall of 1769 where she could impress all the guests with her transformation. The air of dignity that she had acquired during the past weeks was revealed to great acclaim.

As her wedding drew closer, Antoine began to wonder about her husband-to-be. Was he handsome? Was he tall? Although portraits of Antoine had been sent to Versailles and, to her relief, commented upon favorably, she had never seen a likeness of her fiancé. She requested a portrait of Louis Auguste, the dauphin, and after some time, one arrived.

The portrait was an image of a boy ploughing in the fields. It was a classical pose, but it obscured most of his face. She asked for another portrait, and another was sent. The second portrait showed an awkward boy of fifteen with little trace of handsomeness or confidence. Antoine accepted this portrait with tact and asked if she might hang

This pastoral portrait, entitled "The Dauphin Toiling," was sent to the Austrian court not long before the wedding of Louis and Antoine.

it in her room. This act of graciousness did not go unnoticed by the French ambassador.

Antoine was married by proxy in a grand ceremony in the Church of the Augustine Friars in Vienna, on Thursday, April 19, 1770. The real wedding would take place later. For now, her older brother, the Archduke Ferdinand, stood beside her in the place of Louis Auguste. Proxy marriages such as Antoine's were common because of the distance between countries. Legitimizing the couple's union by proxy allowed Antoine to travel with all the luxury and respect of her new status as the wife of the dauphin of France.

As bells rang at six o'clock, the trumpets called everyone to attention. The guests waited while the court made its way from the Hofburg Palace to the doors of the church. All was quiet as the bride approached the altar on the arm of her mother. Antoine looked lovely. Her dress was made from a silver cloth that seemed to shine even in the dimming light of the evening hour. Her face glowed from the rows of surrounding candles as she took her vows and witnessed the blessing of the rings. After the ceremony, the court attended the marriage supper, a feast that lasted several hours.

It would be almost three weeks before the bride would meet her husband. Two days after the proxy wedding, the youngest daughter of Maria Theresa, now "Madame la Dauphine," prepared to leave Vienna. She tried to hide her tears as she said good-bye, but her heart was full. Her mother, who had grown closer to her as they worked day and night to prepare her for her new role, held on to her tightly as though she did not want her to leave. When the bride stepped into the carriage she looked back and tears were streaming down her face. As her carriage passed Schonbrunn Palace, the scene of many happy family moments, the observers that lined the street could hear the dauphine's sobs. She knew it was likely she would never see her mother or her home again. As she journeyed on, the parting words of her mother offered her a little comfort: "Farewell, my dearest child, a great distance will separate us. Do so much good to the French people that they can say that I sent them an angel."

3

La Dauphine

Just before noon on May 7, 1770, Antoine and her cortège of fifty-seven carriages crossed the Rhine River, the boundary between Germany and France. Partway across, they stopped at the Ile des Epis, an island in the middle of the river, where a wooden, castle-like structure had been built. This is where the official transition from Austrian princess to French dauphine would take place. The details had been painstakingly negotiated. An island was chosen because it was the most neutral site possible. The newly constructed building had three rooms: the first one was for the Austrians to receive the princess, the middle room was for the actual ceremony, and the third was where Antoine would become Marie Antoinette, dauphine of France.

In the Austrian room, surrounded by her attendants, Antoine undertook the final preparations. There were many rituals, including one in which Antoine had to strip completely naked and don new clothes brought from France. Here she had to say good-bye to the people who had traveled with her, even her beloved little dog, before entering the handover room. There, after the speeches, Antoine had to renounce all claims to her homeland and her Austrian identity. Once this ceremony was over, Marie Antoinette stepped into the third and final room of the little structure to meet her new household.

In the final room, the emotional Marie Antoinette threw herself into the arms of the comtesse de Noailles, who had been appointed her chief attendant. The comtesse, fiercely rigid in demeanor, drew back. After an uncomfortable silence, Antoinette was introduced to the members of her new household. These women, many of whom had served the wife of Louis XV, were much older than the young dauphine, who was only fourteen and a half. After this initial *faux pas,* even Maria Theresa, who demanded that her daughter always display the poise of a queen, would have been pleased with Marie Antoinette's performance.

The dauphine's arrival in Strasbourg, the first of her stops on the way to Versailles, was announced by the booming of artillery and the peal of church bells. Young girls strew rose petals in the path of her golden coach and little children dressed as shepherdesses and shepherds offered her bouquets of flowers. She waved to those along the route who jumped up and down to get a glimpse of her. In a country ruled by an aging but controlling monarch, Marie Antoinette was a delicate flower, full of

As a result of its location on the border between France and Germany, the picturesque city of Strasbourg is a unique combination of the two cultures.

beauty and promise, bearing the first, slightest hint of the possibility of change.

The city of Strasbourg spared no expense, and the townspeople opened their hearts and their houses in celebration. Orchestras played at crossroads and music echoed all over the city. Exquisite tapestries hung over windows and the smell of oxen being roasted in the town square intoxicated all those whose came to the Place de l'Hôtel de Ville. People danced in the street, the poor were given bread to eat—Strasbourg was putting on a grand spectacle.

Several dignitaries had prepared speeches of welcome, and the dauphine greeted each one graciously. If she felt uncomfortable, she hid it well. In fact, when the head of the

Magistrature came forward to address the dauphine and began to speak in German, she interrupted him politely, saying, "Do not speak German, gentlemen; from today I understand no language but French."

The great cathedral towered above the city, lit from its tallest spire down to the ground. As the celebration continued late into the night, fireworks illuminated the town and barges decorated for a queen stood guard on the river. As this spectacle of sight and sound came to an end near midnight, the young girl, who had not yet met her dauphin, saw their initials entwined in a blaze of color across the night sky. As soon as the firework display faded into the darkness, she was whisked off to attend a ball in her honor. "Our Archduchess," wrote Count Mercy, Austria's ambassador to France, "in her debut at Strasbourg has surpassed all our hopes, as much by her bearing as by the wisdom and unaffectedness of all her remarks."

Marie Antoinette continued to be pampered and indulged on the rest of the journey. Every care was taken that the new bride would feel comfortable and welcomed. The procession included two large wagons, each filled with identical bedroom furnishings. At every stop, after the evening's festivities, she found her bedroom made up exactly as it had been the night before. Each piece of furniture was in its place, nothing amiss, nothing forgotten—armchairs, stools, and screens covered in plush material. Her bed was adorned in satin—scarlet with a white satin coverlet. As she slept, the other wagon, an exact replica of the bedroom she was sleeping in, traveled ahead to the next stop.

Although the people of France seemed to love her, Marie Antoinette was not greeted with enthusiasm in every quarter. Some in the French court were suspicious of the child-bride, whom they derisively called *l'Autruchienne,* which literally means "the Austrian woman" but was also a pun on the French word for a female dog, *chienne.* They feared that Marie Antoinette would be as domineering and politically active as her famous mother. One of the most virulently anti-Austrian people at court was her future husband's tutor and closest advisor. From a young age, the dauphin had been warned by his trusted tutor that he would be married to a woman from Austria who would try to manipulate him, and that he should resist her at every turn.

The dauphin Louis Auguste had been orphaned at an early age. He was brought up in his grandfather King Louis

XV's court. The king was said to be the most handsome monarch in Europe. By contrast, Louis Auguste had a tendency toward obesity and his movements were clumsy. Compared to the magnetic dark eyes of his siblings, Louis's light eyes were often squinted,

King Louis XV, grandfather of Marie Antoinette's husband, Louis Auguste.

due to myopia, and his complexion was pale and washed-out. His manners were poor, he always seemed slovenly, and he dreaded every public function he had to attend. Though intelligent, the dauphin lacked confidence. His favorite refuge from the pressure of court was hunting, a divertissement he loved passionately.

Louis Auguste, as he looked when he first met Marie Antoinette.

Much like Marie Antoinette, Louis had grown up in the shadow of a more accomplished older sibling. In Louis's case, his brother had become ill and, after much suffering, died. As was customary, Louis Auguste was moved into his brother's quarters the day of his death. When his father died, a few years later, eleven-year-old Louis Auguste assumed the title of dauphin—next in line to the throne, a position he never wanted and for which he was ill suited.

Louis and Marie Antoinette were to meet for the first time in the countryside near Versailles. As the bride's carriage approached, horsemen rode out to accompany the procession on the final few miles of its long journey. Crowds lined the dusty road to wave and cheer. King Louis XV and his grandson waited to greet her at the edge of the woods near Berne Bridge. The king, dressed in his fine clothing, looked dashing and debonair, much younger than his sixty years.

As her gilded coach slowed to a stop and two noblemen were helping her down, the dauphine jumped out and ran to the king. She curtsied before him, throwing herself at his feet. The monarch raised her up and embraced her, enchanted with her charm, youth, and spontaneity. He then turned to his grandson and introduced him to his bride. Etiquette called for the dauphin to kiss her, so he kissed her on the cheek.

The young girl's beauty exceeded her portraits. Dressed in the French style, she wore a beautiful hooped dress and smooth silk shoes that showed off her delicately small feet. Her hair was combed up on top of her head. The dauphin, nearly six feet tall, towered over his petite bride. They could not have been more different in appearance. She was pretty and slight and moved like a gazelle; he was tall, heavy, and awkward, almost lumbering.

Among the royal party welcoming the young princess to Versailles were three of the king's four unmarried daughters. Since the death of his mother, Louis Auguste had been close to his aunts. Nicknamed "rag," "grub," and "sow" by their father, Adélaide, Sophie, and Victoire thought the Austrian archduchess represented a threat to their influence at court. The aunts offered Marie Antoinette a tepid greeting. Marie Antoinette would spend most of her time at court

Louis XV's unmarried daughters, Sophie, Adélaide, and Victoire.

with these women, and she knew she needed to win their confidence. The task was a daunting one.

The next day the cortège stopped at the small Château de la Muette in the Bois de Boulogne outside of the capital to spend the night. Waiting to meet their new sister-in-law were the dauphin's two younger brothers. Louis Xavier, the comte de Provence, was the same age as the bride. He resembled his brother in size but possessed a higher degree of self-confidence and a sharp intelligence. Twelve-year-old Charles, the comte d'Artois, was high spirited and animated. He had inherited his grandfather's good looks. Marie Antoinette also met Louis's younger sisters, Clothilde, nearly ten, and Elisabeth, six. Clothilde, like her oldest brother and her Aunt Victoire, liked to eat, and had earned the unfortunate nickname of "gros madame." It was said she was as round as she was tall.

Marie Antoinette of Austria and Louis Auguste of France were married on May 16, 1770 in the Royal Chapel at Versailles. More than five thousand courtiers and nobles of rank received invitations to the wedding. Many more spectators came to view the royal procession, cramming into the Hall of Mirrors on the palace's ground floor. The couple passed through this long corridor, lined with mirrors on one side and doors looking out onto the gardens on the other, on their way to the chapel. For nearly everyone at the palace that day, it was the first glimpse of their future monarch and his queen. The dress of the day was elaborate: elegant, hooped dresses with long trains of flowing material for women; silk coats, swords, and silver buckled shoes for the men. The hairstyles were painstakingly coiffed, ornate, and heavily powdered. Jewels adorned the ladies' necks, arms, and hairdos. The bride herself would spend no less than three hours on her toilette, attended by her ladies-in-waiting, chambermaids, and hairdressers.

This diamond and enamel bracelet was given to Marie Antoinette at her wedding.

On the morning of the wedding a crimson trunk lined with blue silk arrived in Marie Antoinette's rooms. It was six-feet long, three-feet high, and full of magnificent jewels, including diamonds and pearls. The king had included several other gifts: a fan encrusted in diamonds, diamond-studded bracelets with the initials MA engraved on their clasps, and a diamond necklace.

At one o'clock, the spectacle began. As the bride and groom entered the hall, King Louis XV walked directly behind the couple, followed by his family and nearly sixty noblemen. Louis Auguste was dressed in a gold brocade suit embellished with diamonds. His demeanor lacked grace; he seemed nervous and ill at ease.

Marie Antoinette wore a magnificent white brocade gown with hoops on either side that accentuated her slender figure. The soft color of the wedding dress complemented her radiant complexion. She wore the white diamonds she had brought from Vienna and the jewels that she had been given by the king, which highlighted the cool sparkle of her eyes and her captivating smile. In her wedding attire she looked even younger than her fourteen years, "not above twelve." But her regal carriage defied her age. If nothing else, she had the dignified appearance of one who could rule.

Once inside the Royal Chapel, the couple knelt in front of the altar on two red velvet cushions trimmed in gold. The king knelt behind them, as did the archbishop of Rheims, the church dignitary appointed to anoint and crown the French kings. The organs resounded with their music; the archbishop blessed the rings. Louis put the wedding ring onto the dauphine's finger as the king nodded in consent.

The ceremony had lasted for one hour. The two young people, vastly different in so many ways, were now bound together, forever. Historians have made much of the way Marie Antoinette signed the official register. Beneath the

The marriage contract of Marie Antoinette and the dauphin.

dauphin's neat signature, Marie Antoinette wrote her name in a shaky hand. It looks as if she was still unused to writing "Antoinette" instead of "Antoine," and a large inkblot mars

Opposite: The wedding of Marie Antoinette and Louis Auguste on May 16, 1770, in the Royal Chapel at Versailles.

the "J" of Josepha. Certainly nerves can account for some of the flaws in her penmanship.

A sumptuous supper followed the wedding nuptials. Twenty-two members of the royal family sat at the banquet table in the newly-built Opera House and toasted the couple. As they ate, a multitude of spectators watched this ritual from their places in the balconies of the room. Near the end of the afternoon, the skies became dark and a heavy rain fell, making it impossible to continue the planned festivities. The fireworks display was postponed, but the revelry was not over, and celebrations continued for two more weeks.

4

Everyday Life at Versailles

The Château of Versailles is located just outside of Paris, and was originally built in the early seventeenth century. During the reign of Louis XIV, the Sun King, Versailles was transformed from a modest hunting lodge to an enormous, magnificent palace surrounded by two thousand acres of manicured grounds. It had over two thousand rooms, sixty-seven staircases, and twenty-six acres of rooftop and was the most elegant palace in Europe.

The court remained at Versailles most of the year. Marie Antoinette soon discovered that life at court was ruled by enormously strict codes of etiquette. She had to learn three different curtsies for various situations. There were rules about who could speak to whom, who could sit when a member of the royal family was in the room, and who could sit in a wing chair, armchair, or low stools. Marie Antoinette

The royal palace at Versailles is one of the largest castles in the world.

had to learn to whom she should smile and nod, and to whom she should make as if to smile but not actually smile. The complexities were dizzying.

There was a tradition in France that even the lowliest peasant should have access to the sovereign, so court life was a very public life. As long as people were appropriately dressed (they could borrow the necessary finery and accessories at the palace gates), they were allowed almost unfettered access to most of the palace. A large group of nobility had Rights of Entry, which meant they were entitled to be in the presence of the royal family in their private rooms. The rituals of *lever* and *coucher,* for example, as instituted by the Sun King, meant that the king was awakened each morning and put to bed each night in the presence of

THE BUILDING OF VERSAILLES

In the late 1650s, Louis XIV's finance minister, Nicholas Fouquet, built a magnificent château about thirty miles outside of Paris called Vaux-le-Vicomte. Fouquet, an admirer of innovative architecture, employed several of France's most reknowned architects to design a breathtaking palace and hundreds of acres of exquisite gardens.

On August 17, 1661, Fouquet hosted an incomparable party to honor the king and display his new palace. The guests had seldom seen such an exquisite sight, and Louis XIV envied both the house and the garden immensely. Unfortunately for Fouqet, Louis XIV had also recently been convinced that Fouquet was enaged in an anti-Royalist plot and that the grandness of the château was a challenge to the king's absolute power. Three weeks later, the king accused Fouquet of embezzlement and had him arrested and thrown in prison where he would remain until his death in 1680.

Louis XIV, the so-called Sun King, had not, however, forgotten the magnificence of Fouquet's château. He decided to remodel his father's old Château de Versailles into a castle even larger than Château de Vaux-le-Vicomte and make it the grandest palace in Europe.

When the Sun King's father, Louis XIII, had built the first

Nicholas Fouqet's château, Vaux-le-Vicomte, on which Versailles was modeled.

Versailles in 1624, it was a small rectangular building with two small wings and was designed to be used as a hunting lodge. In 1631, King Louis XIII had some renovations done that added three brick and stone buildings that framed a square court, with the front enclosed by an arcade and surrounded by gardens.

Beginning in late 1661, Louis XIV hired the very architects Fouqet had employed to create Vaux-le-Vicomte to renovate his father's castle at Versailles. The major alterations were done within the garden, where the famed designer Le Notre created a huge, symmetrically arranged expanse of flowerbeds, lawns, and statuary.

By 1668, the king was no longer content with the size of the Château de Versailles. He wanted a palace that was appropriate for his extravagant ceremonial and personal life. Architect Le Vau designed the famous Versailles "envelope" that surrounded the current château with new buildings on three sides. This created two faces of Versailles: one for the public, town, and major streets linking it to Paris, the other looking out to the immense private gardens.

The Hall of Mirrors at Versailles.

Despite these grand additions, Louis XIV was still not content. In 1678, another enlargement took place, adding two huge wings that provided accommodations for the entire court along the gardens. With this came the transformation of the terrace created by Le Vau into the famous royal reception room, the Hall of Mirrors. This reception room provided the perfect setting as well as the perfect symbol for the absolute monarchy and the magnificence of the court rituals at the Palace of Versailles.

anywhere from fifteen to one hundred noblemen.

Marie Antoinette's daily routine varied little. She had her own suite of rooms and would wake between nine and ten A.M., be dressed by her attendants, recite her prayers, and eat breakfast. Then she was off to the apartments of her three aunts to visit. If the king were in residence, he might also be there. In spite of their many disagreements, he enjoyed the company of his daughters. The visits usually went on until about half past ten, after which the public day began.

It was the public part of the day that Marie Antoinette at first found upsetting. It was so different from Vienna because what had been private there was quite public at Versailles. In one of her monthly letters to her mother, she described what took place after she returned to her rooms: "At eleven o'clock I have my hair done. At noon, all the world can enter—I put on my rouge and wash my hands in front of the whole world. Then the gentlemen leave and the ladies remain and I am dressed in front of them."

On days when she bathed, the men had to leave, but the women were allowed to stay and watch the dauphine wash. This ritual of the *lever*, which could be attended by anyone of noble rank or name, was extremely disconcerting. This practice of permitting anyone above the rank of commoner to be a voyeur into the lives of the king's family was not at all to Marie Antoinette's liking.

After the *lever* was completed, the dauphine attended Mass with either the king, or her husband, or both. After the service, they would dine "in front of the whole world." The couple tended to eat rather quickly so the meal did not last very long; they would leave the table by half past one in the afternoon. Afterwards, left alone in her apartment, or as alone as she could be with several ladies-in-waiting as constant companions, she read, sewed, did needlework, and even started a waistcoat for Louis XV. Even though she spent her leisure time on this project, her progress was slow: "I hope that with God's help it will be finished in a few years," she would confess to those around her with a glint in her eye. If the vest was indeed ever finished, the king was never seen wearing it.

At three o'clock, the dauphine would pay another visit to the aunts. The king was usually there, but did not stay long, leaving them to their usual banter and gossip about the courtiers. Gossiping was a major pastime at Versailles, one that Marie Antoinette was unaccustomed to from her up-bringing in Vienna. Maria Theresa hated idle gossip and demanded a high level of morality; such conversation would probably not have been heard in the halls of the Austrian palaces.

Abbé Vermond arrived at the dauphine's apartment promptly at four. Her devoted tutor since her engagement to Louis had been negotiated almost two years earlier, Vermond had returned to France with her and continued to instruct her in reading and writing. One hour later, her music lesson began, during which she studied either singing or playing the clavier. By six-thirty, the dauphine worked her way through the secret passageways of the palace to Madame Adélaide's apartment to spend the evening. Even though the miles of corridors at the palace were more or less public thoroughfares, open to any who passed through the great château, the royal family was able to travel from apartment to apartment undetected. Adélaide had given her niece a key to her own rooms so that the dauphine could come and go without an entourage. Having run up and down the staircases and corridors of Schonbrunn as a child at her mother's court, Marie Antoinette was no stranger to the thrill of escaping. From seven o'clock until nine, they all played cards and then had supper.

Late in the evening, the royal family would gather to wait

This portrait shows Marie Antoinette surrounded by her court. *(Château de Versailles)*

The French aristocracy was known for spending their leisure time in elegant salons, gambling, dancing, reading, and gossiping.

for the king's arrival. Marie Antoinette, the youngest, could not always stay awake: "We wait for the King who usually comes at quarter to eleven. While waiting, I lie down on a big sofa and go to sleep," she wrote to her mother. Around eleven, the royals retired to their rooms where the *coucher*, the evening ritual, took place. When the sun rose the next morning, everything happened all over again.

Louis Auguste did not share his wife's enjoyment of gossip and idleness. His days were full of reading, studying and, his passion, hunting. Many days he would leave the grounds of Versailles in the early morning and return only at supper. If he was not out on his horse or in his rooms reading his books or maps, he might be found alongside the palace workmen helping with the painting, plastering, and carpentry.

Often, if the weather permitted, the dauphin and dauphine took walks after dinner in the gardens. These were
some of their rare times alone together. They did not share
living quarters and their interests were different. As they
talked, they slowly began to get to know each other. "I find
my wife charming," Louis acknowledged after several
months of marriage, and went on: "I love her, but I still need
a little more time to overcome my timidity."

Louis was referring to what had become an open secret
at court—the dauphin and dauphine had not yet consummated their marriage. Because they did not share living
quarters, which was typical at Versailles, Louis had to make
his way through corridors filled with lounging nobility and
hangers-on, to visit Marie Antoinette's apartments. Everyone knew the purpose of the timid young husband's visit.
As concern deepened over the dauphin's inability to per-
form his duty and to produce an heir, a secret staircase was
constructed from his rooms to hers to keep the shy dauphin
from having to endure stares and whispered jokes during the
long walk. There was speculation the dauphin or his wife
might have some sort of physical impediment, but a doctor's
examination found them both physically healthy. As more
time passed, the pressure increased, creating a vicious cycle
that led to great consternation in both Versailles and Vienna.
It would be seven years before the marriage was consummated. During all that time Marie Antoinette suffered most
of the blame for not having children.

Maria Theresa, back in Austria, kept close tabs on her
daughter. She followed her daily life with the help of the

loyal ambassador to France, Count Mercy, who arranged a network of spies to keep track of the dauphine. "I have made sure of three persons in the service of the Archduchess," he wrote, "one of her women and two of her manservants, who give me full reports of what goes on. Then, from day to day, I am told of the conversations she has with Abbé de Vermond, from whom she hides nothing. Beside this, the Marquis de Durfort passes on to me everything she says to her aunts."

Armed with the information from Count Mercy, Maria Theresa sent volumes of letters to France. She took Marie Antoinette to task for slips in etiquette, mispronounced words, a stray giggle during some ceremony, but most of all for failing to please her husband and produce an heir for France. The bewildered dauphine asked her mother how she knew so much about her life. Maria Theresa told her it was just a coincidence that her scolding or advice happened to fit an actual occasion so perfectly. It did not seem to occur to the dauphine that someone might be reporting her every move. Despite the pressure and the cruelty of much of the criticism leveled toward her, Marie Antoinette loved her mother as well as feared her. Marie Antoinette felt at times that she was still under her mother's control, even with such a distance between them.

The first trouble Marie Antoinette had with the French court resulted from her efforts to please her mother. Maria Theresa urged Marie Antoinette to introduce a friend of Austria to the French court. But in order to do so, Marie Antoinette needed a special dispensation from the king because she would otherwise be violating the etiquette of the court. When the king, who liked his new granddaughter-in-law, indulged her, the court was outraged. Surely, they whispered, this was proof that Marie Antoinette intended to impose Austrian will on France. To make matters worse, Count Mercy did not defend Marie Antoinette when she came under attack—his loyalty was to her mother. Even after this incident blew over, resentment about the foreign dauphine lingered. She laughed too much, it was said, and was not serious enough to become queen.

The dauphine grew lonely and bored. She tired of the rigidity of court life and wanted more freedom. Her husband was kind, but he essentially ignored her; the king was taken with her youthful charm, but did not spend much time with her; her eccentric aunts were much older than she and not a great source of amusement. She decided that she wanted to go riding.

The empress was appalled. She wrote to her daughter that "riding spoils the complexion" and that "donkeys and horses" occupy "the time needed for reading." Most of all, Maria Theresa reminded her daughter how many women had suffered miscarriages from riding. Once again, Marie Antoinette was reminded of her failure as a wife—she had to write her mother and assure her there was no reason to believe she could be pregnant. Besides, she told her mother, riding would help her to get closer to her husband. She asked the king for a horse and, perhaps because he did not wish to offend the mother or refuse the daughter, or maybe because he had no opinion on the matter, he compromised. A donkey would do just as nicely as a horse. Whether or not

Marie Antoinette on horseback.

Marie Antoinette agreed with him, she accepted the animal. However, in a few weeks, she was riding a pony and soon after that, she was on a horse.

Though Marie Antoinette was accustomed to a life of privilege, she had great compassion, especially for children. Several incidents helped to convince the general public that their future queen was generous and good-hearted. The first occurred when her carriage passed the scene of an accident. She insisted her driver stop, then tended to the wounded man herself while her attendants went for help. She refused to leave until he was safely on his way to a doctor. At another time a peasant was accidentally fatally wounded during one of Louis Auguste's hunts and Marie Antoinette had him taken to his home in her own carriage, and when he died, she made sure his wife and children were compensated.

The public responded warmly to Marie Antoinette's generosity. She was a happy contrast to the reign of King Louis XV, who ruled over a licentious and morally corrupt group of nobles headed by whichever mistress occupied the role of favorite. Louis XV spent money profligately. The nobility and the clergy were exempt from taxation, so most of the money came from the peasants and the burgeoning middle class who lived in the cities and towns. Decades of financial mismanagement had created a dangerously over-drawn treasury. In addition, archaic farming methods meant food was often scarce and expensive.

Marie Antoinette came from the modest, family-oriented Austrian court, where she had lived as one of many children who had grown up under the watchful eyes of her parents. When she arrived in France, she was suddenly treated like a queen in her own right. No longer was she constantly compared unfavorably to her older sisters. Here she was the dauphine—the future of France. Yet behind the accolades and the beautiful dresses, Marie Antoinette was still a fifteen-year-old girl. In Austria, she had her sister Charlotte with whom to spend the days giggling and playing. She had her mother to direct the course of her life and her father to love her. In France, her closest companions were Louis Auguste's aunts, three miserable women who disapproved when Marie Antoinette giggled. Her mother's instructions, once so easy to abide, were now all but impossible for the teenager to implement. She was a failure at everything in

Comtesse Du Barry, a mistress of Louis XV.

her mother's eyes. Worst of all, after a year of marriage, Marie Antoinette was still a virgin. She worried constantly that one of Louis's brothers would father a child first.

In this politically delicate situation, Marie Antoinette could hardly afford to make a mistake. Unfortunately, she could not always avoid doing so. The king, Louis XV, had a series of mistresses, the latest of whom was the comtesse Du Barry. In the French court, it was customary for the king's mistress to occupy a position of considerable power and to be treated with respect by the courtiers. The morality of the situation gave no one pause—it was simply the way things were done. But Marie Antoinette, unfamiliar with this kind of lifestyle and without anyone to guide her, was offended by the king's ever-present mistress and decided she would not acknowledge the woman. She was egged on by the king's daughters, who had reasons of their own to dislike Du Barry.

Marie Antoinette's disdain for the king's mistress did not escape his attention, and his initial warmth toward her turned cool. The aunts urged her to keep up her campaign against Du Barry, but Marie Antoinette began to worry about the king's disapproval. In addition, Louis Auguste's younger brother, the comte de Provence, had recently married, and Marie Antoinette was terrified his bride would produce a child before she did. She knew full well that in a Catholic country, any unconsummated marriage could be annulled and the bride sent away in disgrace. The French wanted heirs, and if Marie Antoinette could not provide them, she would be in trouble.

In the end, Marie Antoinette was left with no choice but to try to mend her relationship with the king. She had to acknowledge his mistress, publicly. It was extremely painful for her to do so, but she managed it gracefully and her position in the court was strengthened. Marie Antoinette soon realized she had been foolish to listen to the king's daughters on this matter—she needed to be more cognizant about where the real power was.

The delicate politics of the French court surfaced again a few months later when international events threatened the Austrian-French alliance. Catherine the Great, czarina of Russia, had invaded Poland and was now offering to divide up the conquered country among some of its neighbors, including Austria and Prussia. The partition of Poland was essentially a bribe to keep the other powerful European nations from supporting a Polish resistance to Russian domination. Though Maria Theresa suggested she did not approve of Catherine's land grabbing, she took the territory she was offered. Then she asked her daughter in France to make sure the French were not upset by her actions. She was worried that France would take Poland's side. Much to Marie Antoinette's relief, the aging Louis XV knew his treasury was too empty to finance a war to protect Poland against vast and powerful Russia. The partition of Poland took place without any objections from France. Had Louis XV objected, there would have been little Marie Antoinette could have done to stop him, which could have made her a casualty of those politics.

In her quest for amusement, the dauphine became intoxicated with the theater. The childhood performances that she and her siblings had put on for her parents brought back happy memories. She longed to recreate that part of her life and resolved there would be a theatrical company, on a much more limited scale, at Versailles. She enticed her two brothers-in-law, Louis Charles and Louis Xavier, and their wives,

Opposite: This painting by Jean-Honore Fragonard, entitled "The Festival at Saint-Cloud," depicts the type of theatrical endeavors Marie Antoinette and her group undertook. *(Courtesy of Art Resource.)*

into forming a small theatrical group. No one but the five of them was to know of the theater's existence. When Louis Auguste was invited to their performances he was sworn to secrecy. Marie Antoinette was certain that the king and the aunts would not approve of such a frivolous endeavor, and no doubt Maria Theresa would be equally dismayed.

The plan worked well for a time. They rehearsed and performed in one of the apartments, where they also designed scenery and made a folding stage that could be hidden inside a large cupboard. The two brothers enjoyed themselves and discovered they had a talent for acting. Their wives, however, could not be counted on for strong performances, while Marie Antoinette's acting talent was passable. The dauphin looked forward to the plays, relishing his part as guest of honor. His applause and enthusiasm encouraged them to write

Marie Antoinette's friend, the Princess de Lamballe.

more plays. To their misfortune, though, they were accidentally surprised by a servant of the wardrobe who entered the room unannounced. Fearful of being found out, the troupe was dispersed as quickly as it had come together.

Marie Antoinette

had been living at Versailles for three years before she went to Paris for the first time. The king did not like Paris, so the court rarely ventured there. But in the summer of 1773, the dauphin and dauphine accepted an invitation to visit. The royal procession was met by military bands and city dignitaries. Crowds thronged the streets. At a banquet in their honor the young couple appeared ten times on a balcony to please the crowds below. A city dignitary remarked: "Madame . . . you have before you two hundred thousand people who have all fallen in love with you." From then on the dauphine could not get enough of Paris. She loved the adoration of the people, the excitement of the theater, and the chance to be away from Versailles. She took with her the one close friend she had made, the Princess de Lamballe, a kind and gentle if slightly dull woman a few years older than Marie Antoinette who had replaced her sister Charlotte as a confidant and friend.

On April 27, 1774, Louis XV suddenly took ill. He had been hunting and complained of extreme fatigue and a headache. He returned to the Grand Trianon, a small château in the vast park of Versailles, and tried to rest. During the night his condition worsened and the next morning he was taken to his apartment at Versailles. Thirteen days later, almost four years to the day since Marie Antoinette had entered France, the candle in his window was extinguished. The king was dead of smallpox. The dauphin and the dauphine fell to their knees. Embracing each other and crying for their loss as well as for themselves, they begged, "Oh God protect us, we are too young to reign."

5

Too Young to Reign

The France that Louis Auguste inherited in April 1774 was neither happy nor prosperous. His grandfather had reigned for fifty-nine years. During those decades the population had grown to twenty-five million people, but there had been no changes to the social structure and little modernization of the government. Most critically, the financial structure of the state was antiquated and deeply unjust. It was the failure to come to terms with this problem, and to make major structural reforms, which led to the revolution that had such tragic consequences for Marie Antoinette and her family.

France was divided into three estates: the clergy, the nobility, and the common people. While the first two estates, the nobility and the clergy, paid few if any taxes, the third estate, the vast majority of the population, was heavily

THREE ESTATES

Many historians cite France's class system, comprised of what were called "estates," as one of the primary culprits of the harsh poverty and injustice that eventually led to the French Revolution and the abolishment of the French monarchy. Because of the extremely unequal treatment of the three estates, millions of French citizens felt profoundly disenfranchised by the existing government.

The First Estate, which encompassed the French Catholic Church, was the most privileged in many ways. The members of this estate, such as the upper clergy and other religious leaders, controlled approximatley fifteen percent of the nation's land and the taxes that could be collected from it. They also collected the tithe, what was usually ten percent of a parishoner's earnings. They maintained all public records of birth, death, and marriages, and operated most of the schools, hospitals, and other institutions that served the poor. All of the First Estate's lands and incomes were tax-free. But the First Estate was not totally monolithic. There was a great deal of tension between church leaders and upper clergy and most of the parish priests, who mostly came from the Third Estate. Many members of the upper clergy lived in Paris or Versailles and did little church work; most were sons of the nobility. The average parish priest lived in the villages or poor urban neighborhoods and deeply resented the gap in wealth and privilege.

The Second Estate, the noble class, occupied the highest positions in the government, military, and often the church. This estate consisted of approximately 350,000 out of a population of twenty-eight million. These people controlled thirty percent of the land and paid virtually no taxes. Their income was derived from a variety of sources, but the basis of their wealth was the rents and dues they collected from the serfs who worked their land. Over the century, as capitalism superseded the feudal system, educated nobles had begun moving into profitable businesses such as banking, insurance, shipping, and trade.

Ninety-five percent of the population, around twenty-five million people, were in the Third Estate. By definition, the Third Estate consisted of anyone who was not in the First or Second Estate. This vast grouping was, as can be imagined, widely diverse. The solid middle of the middle class, or bourgeoisie, such as wealthy merchants and other professionals and intellectuals, were confined to the Third Estate. There were members of the Third Estate who were much wealthier than some members of the nobility, particularly as the economy shifted from agriculture to manufacturing and trade. Sometimes the bourgeoisie would accumulate land and even marry into the nobility, but this social mobility was limited to only the most successful. These men were the most enamored of the ideas of the Enlightenment and the American Revolution. They advocated a representative government and provided much of the leadership for the French Revolution, particularly in its most radical phase. The peasants, who were by the far the single biggest segment of the population, owned around thirty-five percent of the land. The poorest lived as laborers on the land of the nobility and wealthier bourgeoisie. They were squeezed on one side by the inability to materially improve their lives, subsiding as they did on tiny lots of land and laboring for the nobility, and by the majority of the tax burden on the other. They also paid rents, which increased with the rampant inflation of the 1780s, and paid dues on the goods they bought and sold at markets. The urban poor and factory workers were the ones most devastated by this inflation. Over the ten-year period before 1789, the cost of rent in Paris increased nearly seventy percent, while wages only increased twenty percent. It was this latter segment of the population that first exploded with the most violent passion in the months after the storming of the Bastille on July 14, 1789.

taxed. The nobility, which made up most of the court and held most of the political offices, was a powerful force. No French king was so powerful he could ignore the wishes of the nobles. Louis XV had lacked the courage or political skill to convince most of the nobility to share more of the tax burden. The large estates went untaxed.

The church paid no taxes on its vast holdings or on the salaries paid to clergy. Most of the leaders of the church were sons of the nobility, which provided another way to avoid taxation. The church was the biggest landowner in France and many of the peasants bought food and other necessities, such as salt and grain, from the church or the nobility.

The poor and powerless had been abused by an unjust taxation system for centuries. There had always been outrage, but it was the outrage of the weak and presented little threat to the social order. However, things had begun to change by the late eighteenth century.

First, and most importantly, the third estate now included the middle class, or bourgeoisie, who were more highly educated and generally lived in cities or towns and made their living from either skilled trades, as professionals in fields such as law and medicine, or as merchants. Before the modern era the bourgeoisie had been small, but with the increase in trade and beginnings of industrialization, as well as the development of a university system, more sons had left the countryside and learned skills or entered business.

These more highly educated and politically astute members of the third estate had begun to chafe at the high taxation. Why should they have half or more of their income confiscated to support a noble class? Those among the professional class who became intellectuals also began to fuel the conflict and to create a philosophical rationale for social and economic reform. These new intellectuals even

This engraving by Jean Huber depicts an impassioned gathering of Enlightenment philosophers. Voltaire, with his arm raised, seems to preside over the table. Diderot is portrayed to his right.

began to question the ancient doctrines regarding the right of kings, the church, and the nobility.

Many of the Enlightenment philosophers, including François Voltaire, René Descartes, Denis Diderot, and Jean Jacques Rousseau, advocated a doctrine of rationality, in other words reason should be the final judge of what was best. It was not enough to accept tradition simply because it was tradition. It was the moral duty of everyone, particularly the powerful, to use logic and reason when organizing society. Old ways and religious doctrine were no longer sufficient.

The Enlightenment beliefs that all people were capable of reason and should be treated equallyled more people to demand social and economic equality. The stratification of society and the economic burden borne by the peasant class began to seem antiquated and unfair, but most of all unreasonable. It obviously did not provide sufficient income to the state, and was an immoral burden on those less capable of carrying it. Previously, peasants had been taught to accept their lot as God's will. Now, it no longer seemed plausible that God would arbitrarily elevate one man over another.

As Louis XVI came to power, the American colonies across the Atlantic used the ideas of the Enlightenment to justify their rebellion against Great Britain. When the American colonists argued that they should not have to pay taxes because they were not represented in the British Parliament and that there was a philosophical justification to overthrow an unjust ruler, many in the third estate in France listened.

France in 1774 was only a few years away from a catastrophe. The intractable economic and social problems had been ignored for too long. It is tempting to wonder what might have happened if the new king and queen had been more sophisticated and mature. Could the revolution, with its terror and chaos that destroyed so many lives, have been avoided? That is one of history's unanswerable questions. However, they did little over the next fourteen years to avert the political explosion.

Louis XVI became king when his grandfather drew his last breath, but he was not officially crowned until almost a year later. In the meantime, he was very busy organizing his new government. The most important decisions Louis had to make were about his new ministers. Marie Antoinette urged him to consider the candidates she favored, but that plan backfired when Louis remembered his tutor's warning that his Austrian wife would try to dominate him politically. Louis, an intelligent but indecisive man, needed ministers who would provide wise and strong counsel—alas, he did not get them.

When Louis was crowned, his advisors decided that Marie Antoinette would not be crowned with him. The official reason given was that it would make the ceremony too expensive, but unofficially it was clear that the Austrian woman had not earned the trust of the French court. She would have to be content with the role of queen consort. Marie Antoinette, with her typical disinterest in politics, did not protest. She was just happy to be free of the restrictions placed on a dauphine—as queen consort she could go to Paris whenever she wanted and would have a larger income to spend on dresses and furnishings.

Louis XVI's coronation took place at the cathedral in the town of Rheims, the site of French coronations since the Middle Ages. The June day was extremely warm, but the heat did not keep throngs of spectators from crowding into the streets in hopes of glimpsing the new monarch. They came with hopes that the new king would bring about the needed reforms. Poverty was increasing and famine was only one bad harvest away. There was no social safety net in place to help those who could not provide for themselves. When, at the end of the ceremony, hundreds of caged birds were released, the people saw this flight to freedom as a symbol of hope.

The coronation was an extravagant affair. Louis was resplendent in his violet-colored velvet cloak and ermine

King Louis XVI in his coronation robes. *(Château de Versailles)*

cape, embroidered with golden fleurs-de-lis, red-heeled boots made of violet satin, and a white suit of satin cloth. Marie Antoinette looked breathtaking in a beautiful gown of the richest silk embroidered in jewels. Her head was crowned with soft ostrich feathers that framed the pale beauty of her complexion and highlighted her glittering diamonds. During the ceremony, she sat on one side of the altar and watched as her husband was anointed with sacred oil on his head, breast, shoulders, and arms. She listened as he swore the many oaths of his accession and promised to be a just ruler, and she looked on admiringly as he donned a gold crown laden with sapphires, rubies, and emeralds.

It was a solemn occasion, filled with much emotion. Marie Antoinette was so overcome with tears that after the ceremony was over she had to leave her seat for a short time and return to the apartment that had been prepared for her to recover her queenly comportment. As she returned to take her place, she was welcomed with heartwarming enthusiasm. The applause for the queen seemed to be even louder than the ovation for the newly crowned king. Louis, delighted by the cheers of the crowd and touched by his wife's unblushing show of affection, could talk of little else to his courtiers all day long. He returned her compliment with a tender gaze of adoration throughout the rest of the festivities. The royal banquet, where the food was eaten only by the king and about thirty of his guests, was served in front of an audience. Once more, Marie Antoinette did not sit beside her husband but watched from a small balcony along with many other spectators.

After a short rest in the afternoon, the king and queen wanted to meet their subjects. Walking arm in arm through the church square, mingling with those who had waited all day in the stifling heat, the couple was greeted warmly, even enthusiastically. This informal promenade, where they stood face-to-face with the men and women who had traveled far to celebrate the coronation, led the king and queen to believe that these good people of France held them in high esteem. "The anointing was perfect in every way," Marie Antoinette later wrote to her mother; "it seems that everyone was very pleased with the King. . . . It is certain that on seeing people who treat us so well in spite of their misery, we are even more obliged to work for their happiness."

Meanwhile, the new Controller General of Finance was working desperately to shore up France's treasury, but his job was made even more difficult by the royal profligacy. The flip side of the happiness Marie Antoinette saw after Louis's coronation was the rumor that discontent was swirling around Paris. Though the government censored the publishing industry, there was a huge market for the lurid and gossipy pamphlets that were printed abroad and then distributed in the city. These publications ranged from the politically astute, criticizing the king and his court for their excessive spending, to allegations and insinuations of the more intimate and personal kind. Marie Antoinette, the young and pretty dauphine, had long been a target of the so-called *libelles,* but now that she was queen they turned their knives on her in earnest. One of their favorite allegations to make was that the young queen was engaged in sexual activities with a variety of partners, including the king's brother. There was no truth to these claims, but the damage to Marie Antoinette's reputation had begun.

Once named queen consort, Marie Antoinette could choose a new head of her household. She selected her friend

Marie Antoinette's friend, the beautiful Yolande de Polignac.

Princess de Lamballe, even though she seemed to be tired of the princess's quiet manner. Marie Antoinette had recently become closer to a more exciting and engaging companion, a woman named Yolande de Polignac. The Polignac family was of great nobility but equally great poverty. Their association with the queen gave them access to her wealth and gave her, in turn, a reputation for dissolution. The Polignacs formed a clique that was soon well known for expensive card games and other frivolity.

As Louis XVI settled into his reign, Marie Antoinette encountered more difficulties. In 1775, one of Louis's brothers fathered a son. The celebrations only made the queen more conscious of her own reproductive failure. A chorus of peasant women who were, by tradition, allowed to be in the common areas of Versailles, taunted her as she

This painting was made to commemorate the visit of Marie Antoinette's brother Max (far right) in the spring of 1775. *(Kunsthistoriches Museum, Vienna)*

went by, asking when she would produce an heir. Marie Antoinette's younger brother, the Archduke Max (called Fat Max behind his back) came to visit. His poor behavior made for an unpleasant visit, and soured the French-Austrian relationship even more. Marie Antoinette, whose own manners were excellent, was tainted by association.

The queen's sadness and frustration came out one day when the carriage she was riding in narrowly missed crushing a little boy under its wheels. The queen ordered the coachman to stop, then rushed out to comfort the child. When she asked why such a small child had been playing in the road alone, she was told by his caretaker that the boy was an orphan and that she was herself too burdened by poverty and other children to keep a close eye on him. Marie Antoinette offered to take the child to Versailles where he could be brought up in safety and comfort. She also promised to send money for the care of the other children. The woman was overcome with emotion. Marie Antoinette bore a struggling two-year-old back to the palace where he was given over to the care of nurses and courtiers and raised as a child of Versailles.

Adopting a child from the street was not enough. Marie Antoinette wanted very much to become a mother but had little hope of doing so. The queen's despair was widely known—there were few secrets at Versailles—and so, by this time, was the special staircase that had been built from the king's rooms to the queen's, enabling him to visit her without having to endure the stares of the public. It was known that their marriage was not yet consummated, and people began to whisper that Marie Antoinette had taken lovers to try to satisfy her own desires. Pamphlets suggesting the Princess de Lamballe was one of these lovers revealed the growing lack of respect toward the queen.

With no children to care for and no role in her husband's government, Marie Antoinette idled away her days. She took up gambling, a popular pastime, which only worsened her financial situation. She acquired elegant furnishings for her rooms at Versailles, and soon for the Petit Trianon, a little palace attached to Versailles given to her by her husband that was little more than an expensive playhouse. Marie Antoinette spent her days there in the gardens, but always returned to Versailles for her meals and to sleep. More than anything, it represented a hideaway. Louis XVI had his hunting, a passion he indulged almost every day, and the queen had the Petit Trianon. But the little palace became less of an escape when rumors began to circulate that she had ordered it edged

The Petit Trianon, Marie Antoinette's hideaway at Versailles.

in diamonds and painted entirely in gold. Her spending habits were highly criticized, although she was no more extravagant than the other members of the royal family. Her status as an outsider and a queen consort made her more vulnerable to accusations that she was rapidly draining the treasury of France.

On average, Marie Antoinette ordered one hundred dresses a year from Rose Bertin, the most exclusive dressmaker in Paris. The dresses were of the finest materials and designs, including the fashionable addition of stiff side panels to an already full skirt. There were coats, capes, and shoes decorated with jewels to complete the ensemble. She required stylish riding habits and each day three fresh yards of ribbon were needed to tie her peignoir. Two yards of green taffeta came perfectly cut from the dressmaker every day to cover the basket that held the monarch's gloves and fan. When the queen decided to discard her garments, tradition granted that the women of her household could call them their own.

As the queen, Marie Antoinette set the standard for fashion in the most fashionable country in Europe. Her household never stopped inventing new and more enchanting modes of dress, including new hairstyles. In one creation, the hair was swept upward and teased into a grand pouf on top of the head; elaborate and ever-changing accessories were placed within this pile of hair. As these new designs captured the fancy of Marie Antoinette and society ladies, carriages soon had to be made wider to accommodate their skirts, and doorways had to be heightened to allow the passage of poufs.

These are some of the various gown styles that Marie Antionette made fashionable.
(The Louvre, Paris, France)

Although Maria Theresa never visited her daughter in France, the empress continued to be updated on Marie Antoinette's activities through her ambassador, Count Mercy. When he informed his mistress about the queen's extravagant lifestyle, Maria Theresa's earlier concerns turned to foreboding. She knew the people of France could not continue supporting such extravagance forever. In July 1775, she wrote to Mercy, "My daughter is hastening to her ruin."

Maria Theresa's concern was so great that she sent Marie Antoinette's oldest brother, Emperor Joseph II, who had shared the throne of Austria with his mother since his father's death, to France. His visit caused Marie Antoinette much apprehension because she knew that Joseph would, in his stern manner, rebuke her. The lavish and gay lifestyle at Versailles was in sharp contrast to the way people conducted themselves in Vienna. Joseph did lecture her, as she had feared, but Marie Antoinette was so happy to see someone from home that she forgave him. Part of Joseph's assignment had been to investigate the problems the young king and queen were having in the marital bed. He questioned them both and offered some frank advice. Then, finally, after seven years, Marie Antoinette and Louis XVI consummated their marriage.

Just as Marie Antoinette had feared, though, her brother did chastise her in a letter he wrote on the day of his departure. He listed her faults—including her predilection for gambling—and cautioned against her wasted days spent attending the races in the Bois de Boulogne in Paris and the frivolous evenings of entertainment at the opera balls. She should spend more time reading or studying, he said. His letter ended with this thought: "It is time—more than time—to reflect and construct a better way of life. You are getting older and you no longer have the excuse of youth. What will become of you? An unhappy woman and still more unhappy princess." Marie Antoinette was now twenty-one years old.

6

Royal Indulgences

One of the reasons Marie Antoinette's brother had come to France was to remind Louis XVI of the Austrian alliance. Whenever a new ruler took over, there was always the question of whether he would keep the same policies as the previous monarch. Initially, Louis XVI showed no desire to break the Austrian-French alliance, but the death of Elector Maximilian Joseph of Bavaria changed that.

The elector's death caused much excitement among Europe's ruling dynasties because he left no heirs. What became known as the question of Bavarian Succession threatened to cause trouble for Marie Antoinette when her brother, Joseph II of Austria, suggested to the international community that perhaps Austria should be given some of the Bavarian territory. There was no strong leader in Bavaria to oppose him, so it was left to the other countries in the

Joseph II of Austria, Marie
Antoinette's brother.
(Courtesy of Art Resource.)

region to decide whether or not they would allow him to annex part of Bavaria.

As Austria's ally, France was put in a difficult position. France did not want to support Austria's land grabbing. But if they offended Austria, Joseph II could turn to England— France's archenemy—for help. Marie Antoinette was pressured by her brother to exert influence on her husband, but she had little sway over Louis or his advisors. When Joseph II moved Austrian troops to the Bavarian border in January of 1778, anti-Austrian sentiment began to grow in France. Marie Antoinette could only watch and wait, hoping the matter would be settled quickly. The most prominent Austrian in France, she bore the brunt of public opprobrium.

When Frederick II of Prussia announced that he would

take action against Austria if Joseph II invaded Bavaria, the pressure mounted on France to uphold the treaty of mutual defense it had signed with Austria. However, France could not afford a war with Prussia. Although she knew it was useless, Marie Antoinette remained a good daughter and sister and pled with her husband to stand by Austria. Her pleas, though, were to no avail. Tensions remained high for a year and a half until a peace agreement was negotiated to defuse the situation. The Bavarian Succession controversy ensured that Marie Antoinette would continue to be criticized because of her loyalty to Austria, and her motives would continue to be distrusted. It was also clear that she had very little influence over the king.

As the Bavarian problem occupied so much of the court's attention, Louis XVI made a decision that would eventually prove to be immeasurably more important, and tragic. From the first shots of the American Revolution at Lexington and Concord, the French government followed the conflict with detailed interest. Great Britain's victory over France in the Seven Years War had effectively ended French influence in North America. The 1763 Treaty of Paris had forced France to leave Canada and ended a long-running conflict between the two countries over control of North America. The defeat still stung fifteen years later. Many at court, including the king, hoped desperately that the American colonists would defeat the hated British.

The fledgling American congress sent diplomats to France to ask for help. Despite his antipathy toward the British, Louis was initially reluctant. The economic situation was

This encounter between the British and French navies at the Seige of Yorktown was one of the key turning points in the American Revolution. *(Courtesy of Art Resource.)*

worsening, the debt incurred during the last war was still unpaid. His more sensible advisors warned that the treasury could not bear the strain. But under pressure from a wily American named Benjamin Franklin, who was becoming one of the most popular men in France, and influenced by a series of surprising but impressive American victories, Louis finally agreed to help the colonists.

French aid to the American colonists was critically important; without the French navy, for example, the Americans would not have been able to capture the British army at Yorktown and bring the fighting to an end in 1781. But the lasting impact for Louis and his family was mostly negative. Financing the American war effort put an unbearable strain on the French budget. This financial crisis, combined with the inability of the political system to solve the problem , led directly to the French Revolution in 1789.

Philosophically, the American victory, with its rallying cry of "no taxation without representation" and its founding documents, including the Declaration of Independence and

Thomas Paine's pamphlet *Common Sense,* was the first actualization of many of the ideas popularized by such French Enlightenment writers as Voltaire, Rousseau, and Diederot. Suddenly, the colonists in the backwater of North America were organizing a representative government, without a king or codified class distinctions. This new government had promised to be committed to "life, liberty and the pursuit of happiness" for all its citizens, not just a privileged few. There were some in France who pointed out that in actuality there were great disparities in wealth in the new United States, and that slavery existed in a large part of the new democratic republic, but to an increasing number of French men and women, the main lesson learned from the American Revolution was that power could be seized from a king and nobility.

Marie Antoinette concerned herself very little with the goings-on of the revolution in America. She had learned over the past few years what little influence she had in her adopted country. This, however, changed when—after eight years of marriage—she announced that she was pregnant.

Her news was greeted with rejoicing in most quarters, but there were also whispers that the king was not the father of the baby. Louis XVI paid no attention to these rumors, which indicates he was sure of his paternity.

Marie Antoinette's pregnancy was uneventful. On December 19, 1778, she felt the first pangs of labor. The visitors, who had been at Versailles since the second week in December awaiting the event, rushed to get closer to her room. By the time word spread that a possible heir was about to be born, the Hall of Mirrors, the Queen's Antechamber, and the King's Council Room were filled with spectators. Just minutes before the delivery, the double doors of the bedroom opened and anyone who could push through scrambled into the inner chamber. Some made it to the foot of the bed. Two chimney sweeps were so determined to watch the birth that they climbed up on the furniture. They all hoped to be the first to witness the entrance of the new dauphin into the world. Then disappointment—the baby that emerged was a girl. Women were excluded from the line of succession in France; unless a boy was later born to the royal couple, the king's brother, the comte de Provence, would succeed him to the throne.

As godmother, Maria Teresa had the honor of naming the child. It was no surprise when the empress chose the French version of her own name. The godfather, another political choice, was King Charles III of Spain.

Little Marie Thérèse Charlotte was wrapped in blankets and placed in the care of her governess, but not before her father took one look at her and lost his heart. Just as Francis of Lorraine, Marie Antoinette's father, had held his daughter and fallen in love with her at first sight, so, too, did Louis XVI instantly become enamored of his little princess. The proud, beaming new father walked with the newborn into the adjoining apartment to be with her as she was washed and dressed. He then attended Mass to give thanks for this precious gift.

It was difficult to breathe in the bedroom because of all the people. Amid the crushing of bodies and the noise, no one realized that immediately after the birth of the baby, Marie Antoinette lost consciousness. Louis was with his daughter in the next room and unaware of his wife's sudden turn for the worse. When it was finally discovered that the queen had taken ill, several men present pulled the boards off the windows that had been shut against the winter's cold to allow the brisk air into the room. Marie Antoinette's surgeon quickly bled her foot before a basin of hot water even arrived. As the blood flowed from the dry incision, the queen opened her eyes.

Twenty-one cannon shots announced the birth of the royal princess. One hundred and one shots would have welcomed a boy. The celebrations went on as planned, and the king and queen did not forget their subjects in their moment of rejoicing. Money was given to the poor; one hundred young couples were selected to be married by the archbishop, with dowries provided to the girls; wine flowed freely from the fountains in the city's squares and meat and bread were distributed to those in need. Marie Antoinette donated money to her favorite charities. And, following French tradition, when theatrical performances were held at the renowned Comédie Française in Paris, coalmen took their seats in the king's box and fishwives were invited into the queen's royal box.

In early February 1779, the king and queen went to the cathedral of Notre Dame to attend a solemn Mass in their honor on the birth of their baby daughter. Although this Mass of Thanksgiving was usually reserved for a male heir, the couple wanted all of France to share in their joy. But as

Marie Antoinette was an enthusiastic patron of the Comédie Française,which was home to some of the grandest theatrical productions in Europe during the eighteenth century.

the king and queen traveled to Paris, they noticed there were fewer people than expected clamoring to glimpse the royal family in their carriage; nor were the cheers of those who did come as loud and encouraging as they once had been. Louis and Marie Antoinette were not the immensely popular figures they had been a few years earlier.

Motherhood suited Marie Antoinette. She had always loved children and was quietly glad that her baby had not been a boy. A son would have belonged to France, but a daughter belonged to her. Marie Thérèse was a strong, healthy child who united her parents by their love for her. Inevitably, Marie Antoinette's mother and others were soon reminding her how important it was to have another child—hopefully a son that would embody the hopes and the future of France.

With motherhood came a renewed desire to make the French court a more comfortable place to live. Marie Antoinette set about, slowly but surely, making changes to the traditions that had dominated the court for ages. She tried to make court life less formal and to create some

Marie Antoinette began to dress less elaborately after she became a mother.

privacy for the royal family. It did not go unnoticed that her overall goal was to make the French court more like the Austrian one she had known as a child. Though some of the older courtiers were not happy with the changes, Marie Antoinette did gradually give up wearing elaborate and often uncomfortable court dress every day, favoring instead simple gowns that tied with a drawstring at the neck. She kept the color palette she had always used, preferring the pinks, greens, and yellows that complemented her still-lovely complexion, and soon these informal yet elegant dresses were all the rage.

Marie Antoinette filled her days playing with her daughter, enjoying the grounds of the Petit Trianon, and attending and participating in theatrical performances in the evenings. She was delighted to receive childhood friends for a visit, and remained very close to Yolande de Polignac. Louis XVI was said to be happy with that arrangement, as Polignac had a knack for dealing with the queen's occasional moodiness.

Although Marie Antoinette had neither seen nor spoken to her mother since leaving Vienna ten years earlier, Maria Theresa never stopped being a constant force in her life. When Maria Theresa died in 1780, Louis was unable to break the news to his wife. He asked her former teacher and advisor, Abbé Vermond, to tell her. Only minutes afterward, Louis heard his wife weeping. He went into her room and, showing tenderness that touched Marie Antoinette, stayed with her and helped her through her grief. Marie Antoinette had a complicated relationship with her mother and her death brought a mixture of emotions.

Marie Antoinette's grief was lightened when she realized that she was pregnant again. Ironically, the new baby fulfilled Maria Theresa's deepest wish. Louis Joseph Xavier was born on October 22, 1781. This time the baby's birth was not witnessed by the suffocating crowds that had pushed into the queen's bedchamber to watch the birth of her daughter. Yolande de Polignac had taken steps to hide the queen's labor pains, and only those closest to the family were invited into the royal bedroom. The curiosity seekers waited in adjoining rooms. But nothing could keep the news of the birth of a male heir from being broadcast. Pandemonium broke out in the antechambers when the birth of the

It has been reported that upon the birth of the dauphin, Marie Antoinette said, "Take him, he is the State." In this picture he is being decorated with the blue ribbon of the Holy Ghost only minutes after his birth.

dauphin was announced. The king cried; the queen cried; nearly everyone in the public galleries was laughing and crying at the same time.

At the end of the one hundred and one canon shots, all of Paris went wild. Celebrations took place everywhere—there were explosions of trumpets, dancing and singing in the streets, free food and drink, and money for the poor. The capital was lit up for three days as the endless rejoicing gave the country new hope. Delegations of tradespeople were sent to Versailles from Paris to honor the newborn. As the king stood and watched the procession from a balcony of the château, each guild, dressed in splendid costumes with its flags flying and music heralding its arrival, offered a gift that symbolized its trade. Pastry cooks came with special bread for the queen; tailors presented the dauphin with a small uniform made in regimental colors; and shoemakers showed tiny shoes. Chimney sweeps modeled a small chimney on top of which stood a young boy who resembled the sovereign. Butchers led a steer for slaughter, and locksmiths paid special tribute to the king by fashioning a secret lock. When Louis found the hidden spring and pressed it, a tiny dauphin made of steel popped out of the middle. His Majesty, usually awkward at such moments, was delighted at the ingeniousness of these craftsmen. As with the birth of his daughter, Louis XVI went to the cathedral of Notre Dame to hear a Mass sung several days after Louis Joseph was born. Paris greeted him with cheers.

Louis Joseph was not the robust baby his sister had been. His poor health caused his parents worry. It was with much

Marie Antoinette with her three children. *(Château de Versailles)*

relief that Marie Antoinette greeted the birth of a second son, Louis Charles, the duc de Normandie, in March 1785. For Louis, the birth of another boy was met with great delight and relief. Now there should be no question of the continuation of the Bourbon line. For Marie Antoinette, it solidified her role as the mother of France.

But when Marie Antoinette entered Paris two months after the birth of her third child, as she had done twice before, her reception was anything but triumphant. "The Queen was received very coldly," noted a friend. "There was not a single cry of welcome, but a complete silence." Once back at Versailles with the king, she could not stop the flood of tears. "What have I done to them? What have I done to them?" she asked.

Just after the boy's birth, Louis bought the palace of Saint Cloud for his wife. It was a lovely mansion, in a setting of beautiful gardens and fountains, built across the river from the Bois de Boulogne near Paris. The money used to purchase Saint Cloud came from the sale of royal lands and not from the government treasury, which was already in great debt. The people had no way of knowing this, however, and they naturally assumed that more debt had been added to the national deficit for the queen's pleasure. Marie Antoinette wanted the château because the air was considered to be better there than at Versailles, particularly since the five-year old Dauphin's health was still a concern. The family was growing, and to fund the much-needed renovations to their apartments at Versailles would have cost much more than the purchase of Saint Cloud. Regardless, the purchase was unpopular.

Princess Sophie Hélène Béatrice, the couple's second daughter and last child, was born on July 9, 1786. Named for the king's aunt Sophie, who had died four years earlier, the baby was small and weak. In the first few weeks of her life, her health showed little improvement; she did not thrive as those in the royal household had hoped. By the time she was six weeks old, she weighed as little as she did at birth. No grand celebration was planned, most likely because the baby was a girl and was not expected to live long. Sophie died before her first birthday. The royal family's grief over her death was only a taste of the pain and suffering yet to come.

7

The Diamond Necklace Affair

By 1781 France had been supporting the American Revolution for almost four years and the treasury was hemorrhaging money. Louis XVI had appointed a new minister of finance, Jacques Necker, who found some creative ways to fund the massive debt, but his appointment soon fell victim to religious differences: he was a Protestant in a predominantly Catholic country. Necker's loss was a blow; the financial situation worsened.

"Where had the money gone?" became one of the most popular topics of discussion in France. The treasury was empty and someone had to be blamed. Naturally, Marie Antoinette was the most popular culprit. Most of her purchases were easy to see—the elaborate gowns, the elegantly decorated properties, the gifts she lavished on friends, including Yolande de Polignac. When the queen's brother,

Joseph II of Austria, arrived for another quick visit in July of 1781, rumors immediately spread that Marie Antoinette was funneling money out of the French treasury into her brother's hands. Such a thing was impossible, of course—Marie Antoinette did not have access to the treasury. But the rumors indicate how unpopular she was, and how it was assumed she had Austria's interests, not France's, at heart.

The money spent helping the Americans fight Great Britain was not so visible. The ideals of the American Revolution were becoming immensely popular, which meant few French citizens were willing to criticize money spent bringing them to fruition. The volatile situation worsened, and was soon primed for explosion. All that was needed was a spark, which was provided by what came to be known as the Diamond Necklace Affair.

The story of the diamond necklace began years earlier when the crown jeweler, Charles Boehmer, fashioned a necklace meant to please King Louis XV—one he probably intended as a gift for his Comtesse Du Barry. To make the necklace, Boehmer used 647 perfect diamonds. But before Boehmer could finish his creation, Louis XV died. Later, desperate to sell the necklace to avoid financial ruin, the jeweler appealed to Marie Antoinette to buy it. The queen, disliking the style of the piece and unwilling to wear something originally intended for a woman she despised, refused to purchase the necklace. She was also quite aware that it was too expensive. Boehmer continued to press her on several occasions, but she refused to buy it.

Meanwhile, a woman totally unknown to Marie Antoinette

A replica of the infamous diamond necklace crafted by Charles Boehmer.

was scheming to be a part of French society. Jeanne de Lamotte Valois would use any means available to gain the wealth and prestige she thought was her due. She was motivated by a burning desire to avenge what she saw as the wrongs of her childhood. Despite (illegitimate) royal ancestry, reaching back to the Valois family that had ruled France before the Bourbon family, she had grown up in poverty and

Jeanne de Lamotte Valois.

obscurity. Determined to climb the social ladder, she employed her beauty, cunning, and quick wit to try to win entry into aristocratic circles.

One of the men Lamotte used in her quest was the cardinal de Rohan. Born into one of France's great families, Rohan lived an extravagant life, hunting and indulging his pleasures. He had ambitions for moving up in the church, and he sought to charm anyone who could further his career. Rohan was particularly interested in getting closer to the queen, but she disliked him immensely and made no effort to hide her disdain. The queen was put off by the cardinal's immoral behavior and the liberties he took with his office. Lamotte took advantage of the cardinal's desire—in return for money and gifts, she promised him she would help mend his relationship with Marie Antoinette. She showed him letters she claimed had been sent to her by Marie Antoinette. All of the letters were, of course, forgeries. Jeanne went so far as to intimate that the queen was mellowing in her distaste for him and might consider having the cardinal in her court. He was ecstatic. He pushed Jeanne to set up a meeting between himself and Marie Antoinette. She, in turn, had no choice but to go on playing her game of deception.

Jeanne decided to trick the cardinal into thinking he had a secret meeting with the queen. She sent her husband out to find a girl to play the part of Marie Antoinette. He found a prostitute in

Nicole d'Oliva.

Paris named Nicole d'Oliva who bore a striking resemblance to the queen. By bribing various courtiers and taking advantage of the freedom of access the public had at Versailles, Lamotte managed to stage a meeting between the cardinal and the "queen." He was able to pull off this bit of stagecraft because it was well known that Marie Antoinette often took a walk in the gardens in the cool of the night hours. The cardinal was not suspicious when Lamotte told him to be at the Grove of Venus between eleven o'clock and midnight. Soon after the cardinal arrived he saw a woman wearing a white muslin dress, like the one Marie Antoinette often wore, with her face obscured by a headdress. She held

The cardinal de Rohan.

out a single rose, the queen's symbol, and whispered the words he had waited so long to hear: "You may hope that the past will be forgotten."

Another conspirator, disguised as a valet of the court, led the "queen" away before the deception could be discovered. After the meeting, the cardinal felt confident he would be elevated to a place in her circle of intimates. In gratitude, he was only too happy to hand over large sums of money to Jeanne; she assured him that the donations would go to charities chosen by the queen.

The necklace provided Jeanne an opportunity to extort even more money from the cardinal and to hopefully achieve her dream of meeting Marie Antoinette. The crown jeweler Boehmer had been introduced to Jeanne as someone who might be able to convince Marie Antoinette to buy the necklace. After promising Boehmer she would try to persuade her "friend" to reconsider, she went to the cardinal de Rohan and told him that Marie Antoinette wanted the necklace but did not think it was wise for her to purchase it in person. Hoping to further ingratiate himself with the queen, he agreed to negotiate the sale of the necklace himself on behalf of Her Majesty and to guarantee the sale with his own funds. He was told the queen would make clandestine payments on the necklace through him over a two-year period.

The cardinal established the conditions of the transaction with the jeweler before being given the necklace. Then he gave the valuable necklace to Jeanne to give to the queen, and she gave him a contract purportedly written in the queen's hand, promising to make payments. The paper was signed "Marie Antoinette de France." Once Jeanne had the necklace, she gave it to her husband, who took it to London to sell.

As the weeks went by, neither the cardinal nor the jeweler could understand the queen's silence regarding the necklace. The cardinal had hoped to see Marie Antoinette wear the jewels as a sign of her reconciliation with him; Boehmer wanted the public recognition that would come when everyone saw the elaborate necklace he had designed. Feast day after feast day went by and still Marie Antoinette did not show off the jeweler's masterpiece in public. Boehmer even wrote a letter to the queen telling her of the satisfaction he felt knowing that she had the necklace in her possession. When she received the note, Marie Antoinette did not understand what he was implying, so she burned the letter, not giving it a second thought.

Meanwhile, the jeweler was facing financial ruin and needed to be paid for the necklace. He did not wish to approach the queen directly, so he sought an audience with Madame Campan, Marie Antoinette's chief waiting-woman. He told her that he had to have the money owed him and that he had waited long enough. As the queen's confidante, Madame Campan knew of no such necklace and tried to explain that the queen had not made the purchase. Boehmer insisted that the transaction had taken place and suggested that the transfer of the necklace may have been made in secret, without Madame Campan's knowledge.

"Who, then, was her intermediary?" she asked.

"The cardinal de Rohan," was his response.

"The cardinal de Rohan!" she exclaimed, "but the queen has not spoken to him since his return from Vienna. There is no man at the court in greater disfavor. You have been robbed, my poor Boehmer."

When Madame Campan told her mistress the story, the

Madame Campan, Marie Antoinette's First Lady of the Bed Chamber, who uncovered Lamotte's plot. (Château de Versailles)

queen was enraged. She went directly to Louis, who immediately sent for the cardinal. Rohan was brought to the king's chambers, still dressed in the rich robes he had planned to wear to Mass, and interrogated. It soon became clear the cardinal had been the victim of a terrible scam. The king asked him, over and over again, how he could have fallen for such a deception—it should have been clear to the cardinal at once that the letters were forgeries when he saw the signature "Marie Antoinette de France." After a lifetime spent at court, the cardinal knew the queen of France would never sign her name any way but the simple "Marie Antoinette," or just "Antoinette." The cardinal broke down and admitted his mistake. Disgusted, the king ordered the cardinal to be arrested and taken to the Bastille, France's most famous prison.

Before he was locked away, the cardinal took advantage of a distracted guard and managed to send a note to his house instructing them to burn all of his papers. Among the things destroyed was the correspondence between Lamotte and the cardinal that would have definitively proven her guilt; nevertheless, based on Rohan's story, Lamotte and several other conspirators were arrested. The only one to escape was Jeanne's husband, who had fled to London immediately after acquiring the necklace.

The news of the cardinal de Rohan's dramatic arrest spread rapidly through Paris. Stories of the well-known and well-liked priest being tossed into jail, still wearing his robes, captured the public's attention in a way the royal family would soon regret. Once the details of the scandal leaked out, the *libelles* went after the queen. Jeanne Lamotte became a sympathetic figure, portrayed as a woman denied her birthright and unfairly abused by the queen. Other publications alleged that a sexual affair gone wrong had been the cause for the queen's betrayal of Lamotte—some claimed she had been lovers with the cardinal, some with Jeanne Lamotte, and some with both. What was left of Marie Antoinette's good reputation was ruined. It was now painfully obvious that the public was willing to believe the worst about the queen. There seemed to be no limit to the scandalous acts it was assumed she was capable of committing. Although entirely innocent in the Diamond Necklace Affair, public opinion was turned overwhelmingly, and irrevocably, against the queen.

In a desperate attempt to restore her public prestige, Marie Antoinette and Louis XVI asked for a public trial. Her advisors warned her against it. They feared the people had already found her guilty in their minds and that it was better to let the matter be settled quietly. But the king and the queen were determined to have their day in court.

The trial was set for May 1786. The conspirators were tried before the Parlement de Paris, a body of justices eager to affirm its independence from the crown. After a dramatic trial, the cardinal de Rohan was found innocent of any crime, but was banished from Versailles. He apologized publicly for his behavior in the Grove of Venus, renounced his offices, and pledged to donate money to the poor. Nicole d'Oliva, the prostitute who had played the queen that evening, was acquitted because she had no knowledge of the scheme.

Jeanne Lamotte received the harshest punishment. She was stripped naked and flogged in a public square in front of a crowd, then branded with the letter V for *voleuse* (thief). Given a sentence of life imprisonment in the horrid women's prison of Salpêtrière, she escaped nearly one year later and made her way to London where she spent the rest of her life. There, she wrote a best-selling memoir about her time in France, alleging, among other things, that she and Marie Antoinette had engaged in a passionate love affair.

Though the legal proceedings focused on the crime, what was really on trial was the reputation of Marie Antoinette. Perhaps most damaging of all was the court's not-guilty verdict for the cardinal de Rohan. In excusing his participation in the plot, the court implied that the cardinal could have reasonably expected Marie Antoinette to create a secret conspiracy to buy an extravagantly expensive necklace when the national treasury was empty. "The Queen's death," Napoleon Bonaparte later noted, "must be dated from the Diamond Necklace Trial."

8

The Beginning of the End

A year after the infamous trial of the cardinal de Rohan, the sentiment of the crowds in Paris continued to grow hateful toward the queen. Marie Antoinette tried to reform her public image. She turned thirty in November of 1785, and with that birthday made a marked change in her lifestyle. No longer, she told her dressmaker, would she wear trendy, fashionable clothes. She wanted to appear more serious and mature.

Even the shadow of death hanging over the royal family did not stop the rumors. Princess Sophie, born in July of 1786, died in June 1787, and the health of the baby's oldest brother, Louis Joseph, who had been ill nearly all of his young life, continued to deteriorate. While he struggled with these personal tragedies, Louis XVI continued to wrestle, albeit ineffectively, with the financial deficit. But it had been ignored too long. His policies were failing and there were enormous bills to pay but no money with which to pay them.

Louis began to withdraw even more into the distraction of hunting. He purchased the château of Rambouillet because the surrounding forest was full of game. In addition to spending a large sum to buy the property, he decorated it extravagantly. Louis did make a few feeble attempts to rein in royal spending, but it was not enough.

In August of 1786, the Controller General of Finance gave the king a memo suggesting ways he could reform the tax system and improve the poorly structured bureaucracy that ran the country. But like earlier reform suggestions, this one called on the upper class and the Church to shoulder more of the tax burden. Both the king and the Controller General knew that it would be almost impossible to get the Parlement, which was almost entirely made up of nobles, to pass the reforms. The fundamental problem was that the powerful nobility refused to make the tax system more equitable.

Looking for a political solution, the Controller General suggested calling an Assembly of Notables to enact the reforms; in effect, circumventing the Parlement. The king agreed and the Assembly of Notables was opened in February of 1787. Not only did they refuse to pass the reforms the king wanted, they suggested that the only solution to the stalemate would be to convene the Estates General, a body that had not met since 1614.

The king and the rest of the nobility had wanted to avoid

convening the Estates General because they feared the result. First used in the 1300s, the powers of this assembly made up of the three estates had never been clearly defined. If Louis called the first meeting in over 150 years it would be a clear signal that something was terribly wrong. But it might also be an opportunity to try to right the ship of state.

As Louis XVI was struggling with this situation, his closest advisor over the past thirteen years died. The indecisive king relied heavily on the advisor. As the court buzzed about who would now gain the king's ear, Marie Antoinette resisted Count Mercy's suggestion that she try to influence the king's choice. The Diamond Necklace Affair had made a painful and powerful impression on her. The queen told the Austrian ambassador, her mother's old friend and confidant, she did not think it was right for Austria to meddle in the internal affairs of France. As the queen seemed to find strength of purpose she had not previously shown, Louis sunk deeper into himself. He began drinking heavily and seemed even more indecisive than usual.

A new finance minister did his best to curb expenditures at Versailles. He eliminated much of the bloated staff, but Marie Antoinette's reputation continued to sink. By the summer of 1787, she was being referred to publicly as Madame Deficit. A portrait of the queen and her children was to have been hung at a public exhibition but the organizers pulled it from the catalog. They were afraid people would deface it. The queen tried gamely to keep up a brave face. Though she was devastated by the death of her daughter Sophie, she tried to attend more meetings of state in an effort to keep informed about the politics of France.

As the days went by, the crisis in France worsened. There were a series of bad harvests which, along with the financial problems, caused high inflation. The urban poor were often hungry; some faced the possibility of starvation even as they struggled to pay the high taxes. Commoners agitated for tax relief and lower food prices while the nobility blocked the king's attempts at reform. In 1788, the king took the drastic steps of issuing the May Edicts, suspending Parlement until order could be restored. A more powerful king might have been able to use this opportunity to mandate tax reform and

This contemporary cartoon shows a French peasant being crushed by the taxes imposed by the aristocracy.

Jacques Necker.

other fiscal and structural changes that could avert catastrophe, but there was not enough confidence in his leadership to carry it off. Tensions heightened until Louis XVI finally agreed to call a meeting of the Estates General in five years. No one seriously thought he would be able to wait that long. By that summer, the French treasury contained less than a week's worth of money; the need for massive governmental reform was unavoidable.

Under pressure from his wife and others, Louis recalled the popular Jacques Necker to head the Finance Ministry. Marie Antoinette was nervous about the situation, and Louis sunk even deeper into his congenital depression. Their stress was made worse by the dauphin's illness—the boy bore it bravely, but he seemed to be wasting away.

The winter of 1789 was one of the coldest in memory. While the nobility took advantage of the weather to skate and sled, the poor froze to death and starved because of the poor harvest. The king's contentious cousin, the duc d'Orléans, made a public demonstration out of his donations to the poor. He took every opportunity to needle the royal family. When word spread that the king would call the Estates General the next spring, public opinion was, for the first time in a while, positive—people thought that an answer to their problems might be at hand.

In May of 1879, the Estates General was convened at Versailles. The first, and most critical, issue facing this body was how its voting procedures would work. Because the Estates General had representatives from the three social classes, or estates—commoners, clergy, and nobility—there were many more members representing the commoners than the other two classes. If each representative had one vote, the commoners would be in control. This is why the Estates General had not convened for a century and a half.

When Louis XVI had summoned the Estates General, he instructed each member of the Third Estate to bring a list of grievances from his province. The lists were to help the government make decisions about reforms. The implication was that if the Estates General was expected to try to solve the problems of the country, it was necessary that each member be allowed one vote.

In the midst of this political turmoil, Louis and Marie Antoinette had to endure yet another devastating loss. The queen wrote to her brother, Emperor Joseph II, in the winter of 1788: "My elder son has given me a great deal of anxiety. His body is twisted with one shoulder higher than the other and a back whose vertebrae are slightly out of line, and protruding. For some time he has had constant fevers and as a result is very thin and weak." The boy most likely suffered from tuberculosis of the spine and there was little the doctors could do. Louis Joseph did not get better. With his mother at his bedside, the seven-year-old dauphin died on June 4, 1789. For the second time in as many years Marie Antoinette grieved the loss of a child. Her husband mourned in solitude. He felt the loss of his first-born son just as deeply, but could only write in his journal: "Death of my son at one in the morning."

As the royal family mourned the loss of the dauphin, the Estates General continued to argue. Jacques Necker made an official proposal that each representative be given one vote. This was a critical moment. The Third Estate, emboldened by this gesture, declared the Estates General dissolved and called itself a National Assembly and began to discuss a new constitution. This was the first decisive revolutionary move of the French Revolution. With it, the Third Estate rejected the old model and announced their intention of replacing it with a more democratic govern-ment. The privileges of the First and Second Estates were no more.

Three days later, the members of the National Assembly arrived at its meeting place to discover that the doors had been locked. It was assumed that the king was trying to keep the assembly from meeting. These representatives of the middle class, joined by some liberal members of the clergy and the nobility, adjourned to a nearby tennis court to continue their discussions. Soon, by a vote of 577 to one, the delegates had vowed not to disband until they were given a constitution.

The Tennis Court Oath took place on June 20, 1789 and averred that the sovereignty of the people did not reside in the King, but in the people themselves.

The so-called Tennis Court Oath was a radical assertion of authority and a clear threat to the power of the king. The example of the English Parliament and even the defiant stand of the Americans against the English had indicated a path that the leaders of the National Assembly hoped to follow. The time of democratic representation of some sort had arrived. The problem that had not yet been solved was determining exactly what form this new representative government should take. Would it be a Constitutional Monarchy, such as existed in Great Britain, or would the rule of kings and queens be rejected forever, as the Americans had done? The inability to answer this and other fundamental questions would lead to the executions of the royal family, the reign of terror, and the eventual seizure of power by Napoleon Bonaparte.

A week after these meetings, the king, under enormous pressure, shifted his position yet again. At first he had been opposed to the National Assembly, but now he asked it to write a constitution. The king's acceptance of the assembly's authority to write a constitution was an implicit acceptance of their revolutionary acts. It also showed the Parisians and the other kings of Europe that he was a weak ruler. In July, the National Assembly gave itself the power to make laws.

Less than a week later, the threat of food shortages in the capital sent irate citizens into the streets. The rage that had been building was unleashed. The people were ready to arm themselves. The king sent troops into Paris to try to contain the rioting. As crowds assembled near the Palais-Royal to listen to protesters speak, a regiment of the king's troops rushed in and began firing. Panic erupted as the mob dispersed and sought refuge in the quartiers of the city. All the next day and night restlessness permeated the capital. The men and women of Paris began to search the city for weapons. At Versailles, the king and queen had no idea what was happening only twelve miles away.

On July 14, 1789, the people of Paris poured into the streets. Soon Paris was in the grip of an out-of-control mob. Some of them had found weapons but were still without bullets or gunpowder. Then word spread that that the gunpowder they needed could be found at the Bastille, the state prison. The crowds made their way to the eastern part of the city where the symbol of governmental oppression stood.

The soldiers protecting the prison began firing into the crowd, killing nearly one hundred people and wounding seventy-three others. After several hours of fighting, the mob stormed the prison, seized what ammunition they could find, and freed the seven prisoners locked inside. The attackers then led the prison governor and the soldiers to the nearby Hôtel de Ville. On the way, the governor was assassinated and some of the troops were killed. The heads were placed on long spears and a

The storming of the Bastille prison on July 14, 1789 continues to this day to be celebrated in France as the beginning of French democracy.

horrific procession paraded through the streets of Paris.

Meanwhile, the royal family at Versailles spent the day as any other, unaware of what was taking place in Paris. Marie Antoinette went about her toilette and Louis remained in bed, choosing not to go hunting. When the king was told of the storming of the Bastille, he seemed unconcerned. Thinking it a small protest, he remarked: "But this is a revolt." The messenger replied somberly, "No, it is a revolution."

The next day the king went before the National Assembly. Back in Versailles, the queen insisted those closest to her should flee. Those sent away included Marie Antoinette's confidante Yolande de Polignac and the king's brothers. Though it was difficult for the queen to see her friend go, she feared for her safety. No one knows for certain why Marie Antoinette did not accompany Polignac to Switzerland, but it was probably because she did not want to leave her family behind.

Now, the tiny tricolor ribbons of red, white, and blue that symbolized the revolution were seen everywhere in Paris. The king even allowed one to be tucked into his hat. The duc d'Orléans wore his proudly, infuriating Louis. Even more upsetting was the *grande peur,* or great fear, that swept the country during the summer of 1789. There were revolts throughout the countryside and riots in the capital on an almost-daily basis. The king and queen stuck close to Versailles, trying to keep a low profile. Though some of their advisors urged them to leave, they did not. Later, the king would say, "I know I missed the opportunity. I missed

During the peasant revolutions, many commoners looted and pillaged rural châteaus and destroyed the records of their signeurs, prompting the new National Assembly to abolish feudalism once and for all.

it on July 14. That was the time to leave and I wanted to."

As summer turned into fall, life at Versailles went on, if a little more subdued than usual. The king continued to hunt as often as he could, and the queen occupied herself with her needlework and her children. In October, the king gave a dinner for his troops to reward their loyalty. The king and queen had not planned to attend, but as the evening wore on, the soldiers, fueled by wine, began to demand their presence. The royals obliged. The next day, the papers were quick to report that the night had turned into an orgy of alcohol and royalist statements, and that the tricolor had been removed from many a costume and thrown on the ground in disgust. These reports were no doubt exaggerated, but they infuriated the Parisians, who were still facing food and fuel shortages. On Monday, October 5, an angry mob of market women set out for Versailles. Marching the twelve miles from the capital to the palace, the women had plenty of time to stir up their rage. They were concerned about political, economic, and social issues, but most of all they wanted to vent their anger. For months they had been struggling to feed and clothe their children while, from their perspective, the king and his immoral Austrian wife were living in luxury, unconcerned about anyone else's suffering.

When word of this unusual procession arrived at Versailles, the royals were called together for a quick conference. They could not agree on the best course of action. Some favored flight, others wanted to stay, and even the questions of where to go and how to get there could not be answered. Again, Marie Antoinette refused to leave her husband, who dithered without making a decision. When the market women arrived at the palace, the royal family was still there. The king agreed to meet with one representative of the marchers and promised her they would be given bread. Though they had met with the king, the people were still angry and restless. An apocryphal story has it that the duc d'Orléans marched among them disguised as a woman, urging the crowd to violence. As night fell, they remained in the courtyard.

Few people slept that night at Versailles. Just before dawn, the market women attacked. They rushed into the palace and made for the queen's rooms, shouting "Hang the Queen, and tear her guts out!" Marie Antoinette managed

À Versailles À Versailles. *du 5. Octobre 1789.*

This contemporary drawing depicts the procession of angry market women. The accompanying caption reads "To Versailles! To Versailles!" *(Musée Carnavalet, Paris)*

to escape down the secret staircase that led to the king's rooms but the mob killed two of her bodyguards. A few hours later, the king and queen were called out onto a balcony. In an attempt to appear more sympathetic before the women of France, Marie Antoinette tried to bring her children with her, but shouts from the crowd sent the children back inside. The monarchs trembled as they stood, not knowing if an assassin's bullet would be their fate. Instead, the mob decided to bring them back to Paris.

The royal family was loaded into a coach and taken, in a long and slow procession, from Versailles to the Tuileries palace. As they traveled, the women shouted triumphantly, "We shall not need bread now. We are bringing the baker, the bakeress and their little brat." The Tuileries, originally built by Catherine de' Medici in the sixteenth century, had

123

Marie Antoinette's friend and probable lover, Count Axel Fersen.

not been used in years; it was in disrepair and filled with squatters. Nevertheless, the royal family was lodged there, uncertain as to whether they were prisoners or not. They were allowed to keep most of their households with them, comprising several hundred people, and to continue in most of their day-to-day activities, but they were not free to leave.

During this confusing time, the queen was comforted by the nearness of her friend Count Axel Fersen. A Swedish aristocrat who greatly admired the queen—and with whom it is assumed she had a sexual affair—Fersen took apartments nearby and visited often, bringing news and reassurances. He was also acting as an unofficial observer for the Swedish government. All of Europe's attention was trained on France and every government feared that the revolutionary fever would spread.

What followed was weeks of idle waiting punctuated by episodes of nerve-racking activity. The National Assembly tried to write a constitution, which would determine the king's role in the new system. The Declaration of the Rights of Man and Citizen had been read and accepted in August. Based loosely on the American Declaration of Independence, this document gave all power to the people and was designed to right the wrongs perpetrated by the previous system of rule. It was becoming clear that if Louis XVI kept any power, it would be very limited. As the world waited and watched, the sympathy initially felt for the king began to turn to contempt as he failed to engage in the events that determined his future and that of his family's. He spent most of his time hunting.

The political change that offended the king most deeply was the Civil Constitution of the Clergy. One of the main premises of Enlightenment philosophy, from which much of the revolution drew inspiration, was that the church should not have authority over man. Accordingly, the National Assembly set out making the Catholic Church subservient to the state. It created a civil constitution that all priests were required to sign (though only a little more than fifty percent of them did) and forced the Church to turn over all of its lands to the state. Those priests that stayed loyal to the Catholic Church after the pope rejected the civil constitution had to flee or go into hiding.

Louis and his family were deeply religious and saw the civil constitution as an egregious wrong. As Easter of 1791 approached, it became clear that Louis would have to attend Mass and take communion from a juror priest (one who had signed the oath). Louis's elderly aunts were so against doing this that, after some difficulties, they managed to flee to

Rome. For some time, Marie Antoinette and her husband had been quietly discussing a flight of their own. Now, that flight seemed their only option.

Plans for their escape began in December of 1790, but the attempt did not take place until June of 1791. The queen wanted to wait for assurances from abroad, especially Austria, that they would have support if they arrived in those countries, but those promises were slow in coming. Finally, with Fersen's help, the royals procured a carriage, and on June 20, 1791, they fled the Tuileries. They took their two children, the king's sister Elisabeth, and the children's governess, and headed for the town of Montmédy, one hundred eighty miles to the east, near the border.

The escape was troubled from the start. The king and queen were unaccustomed to making secretive plans for midnight carriage rides across France. They were unaccustomed, in fact, to even stepping into carriages without a platoon of footmen to help. Not one of the adults in the vehicle proved adept at making good, quick decisions. Between their bumbling and a few other minor glitches and miscommunications, they were gone less than twenty-four hours before the king was recognized. Troops were alerted, and the royal family was captured and brought back to Paris in disgrace. An order had been given that they were to be neither applauded nor insulted along the route, and though the streets were lined with spectators, the coach containing the monarchy of France traveled in near-total quiet. Only an occasional cry broke through: "Long live the Nation!" It was an ominous return.

In the fall of 1791, France officially became a constitutional monarchy. The king accepted the new constitution without complaint—at least, in public. He and the queen were terrified to speak against the changes in public, but in private they could share their distress. As the slogan "Liberty, Equality, Fraternity" was shouted through the streets of Paris, their only hope was that

This poster contains the new slogan of the government, accompanied by the emblematic tricolor flags and red cap.

some foreign power would come to save them. When Marie Antoinette's brother Joseph II died, her younger brother, Leopold II, replaced him. Though the two had never been close, the queen begged him to use his diplomatic power to effect her family's release. As she spent all her free moments scribbling letters to anyone she thought might help them, Marie Antoinette was forced to spend her public hours acting like the queen of France. Under duress from the new government, she was forced to recall her household from exile, including her beloved friend Lamballe. The new court went about its business warily, always on the alert for signs of disapproval.

The French Revolution had initially found sympathy abroad, as it was seen as a triumph of the people. But as the months wore on, that sympathy turned to distrust. The revolutionaries came under the control of the most radical faction, called the Jacobins because they met at a club near an old convent with that name. The more radical leaders were intent on spreading their beliefs across Europe, and they declared war on Austria in April of 1792. The declaration of war was given to Louis XVI to read publicly; he did so with great reluctance. In the meantime, Marie Antoinette's brother Leopold had died and leadership of Austria was given to Leopold's son Francis II. Though they had never met, Marie Antoinette did her best to help Austria during this war. She even sent him news about troop movements and battle plans.

Part of the new powers granted to Louis XVI under the constitution was the power to veto measures passed by the National Assembly. Those members provoked him by passing measures he had to veto to avoid looking like a mere tool of the assembly. Each veto made Louis more unpopular with the people of France. Marie Antoinette's old nickname, Madame Deficit, was replaced with a new one—Madame Veto. As usual, the people unhappy with the government made her the scapegoat.

As popular sentiment continued to turn against the queen, the royal family nervously awaited the twentieth of June— the one year anniversary of their intercepted flight from Paris. Much as they had feared, the day brought an angry mob to the Tuileries. The queen had to be convinced to leave her husband's side because her presence might enrage the people further. As it was, they brought down doors with hatchets, surged through the palace, and forced the king to don the red cap of the republicans.

This experience made the royal family even more apprehensive about the upcoming anniversary of the storming of the Bastille, on July 14. Marie Antoinette faced more pressure to flee France, but she again refused. There was room for a little hope. Prussia had entered the war on Austria's side and the queen hoped that troops would arrive in time to rescue her and her family. Bastille Day passed without any actual violence, but it was clear the people were agitated. The *sans-culottes,* revolutionaries named for their habit of wearing long pants instead of the breeches of the upper classes, were hungry for more revolution. By this point the revolution had taken on a life of its own. The worst charge a member of the assembly could suffer was to be accused of not having sufficient belief in the revolution. The *sans-culottes* were particularly virulent in their determination to push forward so there was no chance the old system could be restored. More and more people began to speak of the importance of overthrowing unlawful rulers—and this time, they meant the king. As the political situation continued to develop, rumors flew that the Tuileries would be attacked. On the morning of August 9, 1792, word came that the attack would be that night.

Hardly anyone slept as nearly ten thousand people gathered around the palace. At dawn, the king made an attempt to review his troops, to show the crowds he was unafraid. They just laughed at him. The royal family was protected by a regiment of fanatically loyal and highly trained Swiss

Guards but, given the size of the opposition, no one knew if they would be able to hold the palace. After much intense discussion, the king and queen were convinced to go to the National Assembly and present themselves to that body. Once there, they were kept in a holding area for more than ten hours while the assembly debated their fate. Less than two hours after they left the Tuileries, a massacre occurred.

No one can say who fired first, but as the people crowded around the palace, the Swiss Guards held their posts until, suddenly, shots rang out and the melee began. For several hours, people fought and killed each other throughout the blood-soaked palace and grounds. The blood lust was released unchecked; the carnage was horrific. Afterward, the National Assembly decided to suspend the king's powers pending a final resolution made by a national convention

Rioters took over the Tuleries in the presence of the king and queen on August 10, 1792. *(Courtesy of Art Resource.)*

The royal family was held at the Temple from 1792 on.

of elected citizens. A few days later, the king and his family were taken to another old palace called the Temple. This medieval tower was, unequivocally, a prison.

Now imprisoned in the small tower, their lives changed drastically. Louis was allowed only one valet while the rest of the servants were dismissed. Spied on constantly by guards, their every move was observed. To pass the time, Louis instructed his son in reading, writing, and Latin; he also tried to pass on his love of geography and history to the boy. Marie Antoinette and Louis's sister Elisabeth spent many hours knitting, doing needlework, and helping Marie Thérèse with her music lessons. They were permitted to walk in the gardens on certain days, savoring the fresh air and change of scenery. A few people loyal to the old regime smuggled news to the royal family, including reports that the Prussian army had entered France. The weeks passed, and still, they never gave up hope that they might be saved.

Several of the royal attendants, including the Princess de Lamballe, Marie Antoinette's closest friend, had also been imprisoned. Royalist sympathizers were being jailed almost every day, and the public remained frenzied. At the beginning of September the prisons were stormed again and as many as two thousand people were murdered by the citizens of Paris. Among those killed was the Princess de Lamballe, who was raped and mutilated before being decapitated. Her head was mounted on a pike to be paraded through the streets of Paris. The crowd wanted to show the head to the queen, knowing how much she loved her friend, but first took it to the hairdresser to ensure Lamballe's signature blond curls would be recognizable. Though the queen did not see Lamballe's head as it bobbed outside the Temple window, the story of the spectacle could not be kept from her and it was a painful blow. Princess de Lamballe had been murdered because of her association with the queen.

Paris remained out of control. The killing stopped, but the looting continued—even the crown jewels of France were stolen. Unsurprisingly, Marie Antoinette was accused of having masterminded this crime from behind her prison bars. But one advantage of life in prison was that the royal family heard very little from the outside world. In fact, life in prison was in many ways more comfortable and pleasant than life at Versailles had been. Though their freedom was severely curtailed, the little family was together. They spent the days in a regular routine, walking together in the gardens (so the guards could search their rooms), playing cards in the afternoon, and being read to by the king in the evenings. Each night around dusk a group of criers took up position near a window and shouted the day's news. This was how the royals learned, on September 21, that the monarchy had been abolished and that the National Convention, an elected body, was now in charge of the new French republic.

The abolishment of the monarchy meant it was now forbidden to use the titles of the *ancien regime* (old regime). Louis and his family were now referred to as the Capets, the name his ancestors had used hundreds of years before. Even crowns embroidered on the king's underclothes had to be picked off. The duc d'Orléans became Philippe Égalité and, so far, seemed to be riding a tide of goodwill for his opposition to the king.

Once the monarchy was abolished, something had to be done with the former royals. They could not be left in jail indefinitely, but the National Convention could not agree on the proper course of action. As they debated, the former king and queen could do nothing but wait. The tide of the war had turned against the Prussian invaders. As the French armies scored victories over the Prussians, the possibility of rescuing the royal family seemed more remote. A few weeks after the king was removed from his throne, the decision was made to try him for treason. In October, he was separated from his family and placed in an isolated cell.

Louis was formally charged and given access to lawyers to help him prepare his defense. He was faced with the cruel choice of leaving his children with his wife or keeping them himself. Knowing how it would hurt Marie Antoinette to have to give them up, he told his guards to leave the children with her. The former king spent the last weeks of his life with his papers and his lawyers. His family wept and prayed,

After he was formally charged with treason, Louis XVI was held in solitary confinement at the Temple. *(Courtesy of Art Resource.)*

unable to communicate at all with their patriarch and not knowing what further horrors might lie in store. The former king was allowed to write a will, which he signed, defiantly, as Louis XVI. In it, he showed the strength of a man with nothing left to lose. He asked his son, should he ever inherit his father's crown, to treat his subjects kindly and not seek revenge. His told his wife that he loved her and that he was sorry if he had brought her any unhappiness. Despite the difficult times they had encountered, despite the people who

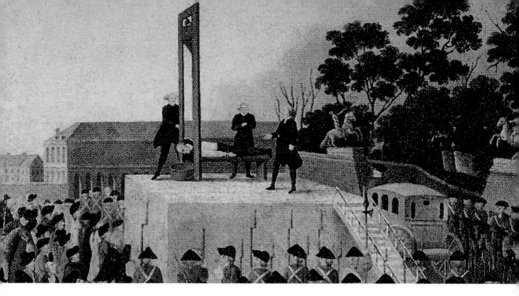

The execution of Louis XVI by guillotine in the Place de la Révolution, earlier named Place Louis XV in honor of the king's grandfather.

had tried to pull them apart, Louis and Marie Antoinette had come to understand and love one another.

On January 16, 1793, Louis Capet was found guilty of treason and sentenced to die by guillotine in the public square of the Place de la Révolution. Among those in favor of this ultimate punishment was the former duc d'Orléans, who would eventually suffer the same punishment himself. (As Orléans later walked to his own beheading, cries of "I vote for death!" mocked his betrayal of the king.)

On January 20, 1793, Louis was reunited with his family for the evening. It was a terrible time; everyone present knew the king would die the next morning. Marie Antoinette begged her husband to stay with the family overnight but Louis refused—he had, he said, to prepare himself. She allowed him to leave only after he promised he would return in the morning, a promise he did not keep. Just after ten A.M. the next day, the family heard the sound of the drums and then the roar of the crowd that meant the king was dead.

9

The Queen's Last Days

Louis's death devastated Marie Antoinette. She was given his wedding ring and allowed to wear mourning clohes, and she let her grief consume her. Elisabeth had to keep the family together as best she could. Marie Antoinette refused to eat or to leave her room because she would have to pass the door to the apartment where Louis had spent his final days. While those abroad argued about whether Louis Charles should be considered Louis XVII and if so, who his regent would be, Marie Antoinette turned a deaf ear to everyone and everything. Though she was not yet forty years old, her hair turned white and she had the pallor of a woman twice her age.

Life in the Temple dragged on. The death of the king seemed to have placated the French people for the time being, and it seemed possible that Marie Antoinette and her family would be sent to Austria in an exchange of prisoners. They sat in the tower, waiting for news. Marie Antoinette might not even have known about the multitude of plots to break her out of jail that either failed or were abandoned. Austria was not committed to her res-

Louis Charles, the would-be Louis XVII.

cue—the plotting was left to various individuals still sympathetic to the royal family.

Internationally, France was energized by its victories against Austria and Prussia and declared war on England, Holland, and Spain. It was an overstep propelled by enthusiasm, however, and the tide began to turn against France. As the French armies reeled, a prominent Jacobin named Maximilien Robespierre devised a plan he hoped would recharge the will of the people of France. He suggested that Marie Antoinette also be brought to trial for treason.

Eight-year-old Louis Charles was taken from his mother in July 1793. Marie Antoinette fought the guards with all her energy, but she could not stop them. She became obsessed with trying to glimpse a bit of her son through the bars over her windows. At the end of the month, she was taken in the middle of the night and placed in the dungeon of the Conciergerie, along the Seine River. This dungeon was known as the chamber of death. Marie Antoinette never saw her son or daughter again.

MAXIMILIEN ROBESPIERRE

"Terror is nought but prompt, severe, inflexible justice; it is therefore an emanation of virtue; it is less a particular principle than a consequence of the general principle of democracy applied to the most pressing needs of the fatherland." So spoke Maximilien Robespierre, the man who came to embody the so-called Reign of Terror that hastened the execution of the French monarchs and many members of the French aristocracy.

Robespierre was a young lawyer from the town of Arras who was elected to the Estates General in 1789. After coming to Paris, the gifted *avocat* gained prominence within the Jacobins, the more radical members of the Estates General and the new National Assembly. He was a powerful speaker, and his devotion to the political and religious ideas of Jean Jacques Rousseau, particularly his emphasis on personal and civic virtue, soon gained him the nickname "The Incorruptable."

Robespierre's relentless emphasis on the "will of the people" and "civic virtue," made him a progenitor of modern totalitarianism. When the Austrians and other European nations aligned against France in an attempt to end the revolution in 1792, the revolution became more extreme. Robespierre led the fight against those who sat on the right side of the National Convention—giving birth to the modern notions of the political right and the left—and helped to put the Jacobin "left" in power. He advocated for the execution of the king.

After the purging of his political opposition in January 1793, Robespierre was elected to the Committee of Public Safety. This peak of his political power coincided with the Reign of Terror. As the all-powerful Committee of Public Safety split into right and left factions, Robespierre found a place between the warring groups. From the temporary safety of the middle, he was able to have the leaders of the right—Georges Danton—and the left—Jacques Herbert—arrested and beheaded on the newly invented guillotine in the months of March and April of 1793.

In the process of dispatching his political opponents, however, Robespierre soon discovered that he had himself run out of favor. His power had grown to such a level it began to frighten many of the same men who had once been his main supporters. Facing divisions within the committee, he attempted to carry the day by threatening to purge his opponents. They reacted by arresting him that night, July 27, 1794, and beheading him the next morning. In the twentieth century, many historians, particularly Marxist historians, came to think that the overthrow and death of Robespierre was the climax of the French Revolution.

The Conciergerie was another former palace renovated to serve as a prison. It was attached to the building in which the Revolutionary Tribunal met; doomed prisoners moved in and out in a ceaseless flow. Marie Antoinette's cell was open along one wall, so anyone who cared to could stop and stare in at her. She was kept alone, though she was allowed an attendant, a young girl named Rosalie who greatly admired the former queen's bravery and kindness in the face of all her troubles. Rosalie did her best to make her prisoner more comfortable but there was very little she could do. Despite these privations, Marie Antoinette was gracious—she maintained her famous composure until the very end.

Denied the comfort of her needlework, Marie Antoinette passed her time reading or watching her guards play games of cards. Again, several plans were made to try to free her, but the only one that got very far was the so-called Carnation Plot. One day, a man dropped a carnation onto the floor of the former queen's cell. Tucked into its leaves she found a tiny note describing a plan for rescue. A guard gave the plot away before anything could be accomplished, but it gave Marie Antoinette's enemies the excuse they needed. She was interrogated at length for several days and handled the questioning brilliantly. She gave nothing away and managed not to incriminate anyone, including herself. Her performance was in vain, however—though she did not know it, her death sentence had already been decided.

Revolutionary leaders swayed by Robespierre agreed to sacrifice Marie Antoinette to their cause. They hoped her death would unite the *sans-culottes* behind them and show their enemies abroad that they would not hesitate to take drastic measures. Their plan was aided by a terrible accusation. Young Louis Charles, who had spent nearly half his life in prison and had been separated from his family for several months, was coerced into alleging that his mother and his aunt had sexually abused him.

In early October 1793, the former queen was brought before a secret meeting of the Revolutionary Tribunal. All the old, baseless charges were brought up again—that she had funneled money from the French treasury to her brother Joseph II, that she had had numerous adulterous affairs including with Princess de Lamballe, and that she had induced her husband to try to escape from the Tuileries in June of 1791. Marie Antoinette denied everything. She was given a lawyer but had only a few hours to prepare a defense. Her official trial began two days later in an open courtroom. The building was mobbed by people curious to see the once-haughty queen brought to her knees.

Marie Antoinette's face was pale against her black mourning dress, and her widow's bonnet made her look old beyond

Marie Antoinette during her trial. *(Musée Carnavalet, Paris)*

her years. Over two long days, forty-one false witnesses testified against her. The most damaging testimony was the one suggesting she had sexually abused her own son. Throughout the trial the former queen responded to the other accusations quietly and firmly. This charge, though, roused her to passionate speech. She took to her feet and appealed to the women in the courtroom as mothers, saying she could never have done such a thing to her child. The tribunal listened impassively, though some spectators were moved to tears by the sight.

In the end, the intent of the trial was not to convince the tribunal of her guilt—that had already been determined— but to paint a final portrait of Marie Antoinette as an evil, scheming, manipulative woman. On the fifteenth of October, she was declared guilty of high treason and sentenced to death. Offered the chance to speak, the former queen could only shake her head. It was all she could do to keep her chin up as her jailers led her away.

The following morning, Marie Antoinette was forced to dress herself in front of her guards. Rosalie tried to offer her some food, but she would not eat. In a final indignity, she was denied the right to wear her mourning clothes and had to don her only other dress—a simple white shift. No one present could have known that many years ago the queen of France would have worn white to mourn.

A gendarme stood guard as she knelt to pray. The judges arrived in her cell and read the death sentence for the second time. Her hands were then bound and the executioner arrived to cut off her hair. She was allowed to don a bonnet

Marie Antionette being led to the Place de la Révolution for her execution.

for the journey to the execution site and was then led outside to the cart that waited for her. The formerly beloved queen was made to sit backwards as the wagon rolled toward the scaffold. The journey to the Place de la Révolution lasted nearly one hour. Her ears rang with the jeers of the crowd that had come to see her die: "Vive la république! Vive la nation!"

At the scaffold, Marie Antoinette got out of the cart. Twenty-four years earlier, she had entered France in triumph—the young dauphine, the symbol of the future. Now, she kept the dignity and regal bearing for which she had so long been known as she stepped up to the executioner's platform. The drums beat their ominous roll of death and the bloodthirsty crowd cheered, clamoring for Marie Antoinette's severed head. As she walked toward the wooden collar of the guillotine, she stepped on the executioner's foot and, in response to his show of anger, murmured, "Monsieur, I ask your pardon. I did not do it on purpose." Without any further ceremony, Marie Antoinette became another victim of the revolution.

Louis Charles would not live to take his father's throne. He died at the age of ten, while still imprisoned, from tuberculosis. Marie Antoinette's execution began a wave of bloodshed, led by Robespierre, that became known as the Reign of Terror. Louis XVI's sister Elisabeth was executed in 1794. Marie Thérèse was exchanged for Austrian prisoners-of-war in 1795 and lived a long, if unhappy, life in exile.

The Reign of Terror ended with the execution of Robespierre, but the violence had left France internally unstable and internationally loathed. Much of the world had turned away in disgust as the French Revolution became an orgy of incrimination and violence. Finally, in 1799, a Corsican military officer, Napoleon Bonaparte, overthrew the government. In 1804, he had himself proclaimed the hereditary emperor. He established a strong centralized government and almost single-handedly redrew the map of Europe through a series of wars. For a brief time, France was the master of most of Europe. After Napolean was forced from power, he was replaced by the former comte de Provence—Louis XVI's brother who had gone into exile before the revolution. Now Louis XVIII, he arranged for the remains of his brother and Marie Antoinette to be restored

This painting by Jacques-Louis David shows a romanticized Napoleon crossing the Alps on the way to his conquest of Italy in 1796. *(Kunsthistorisches Museum, Vienna)*

to their rightful place in the church of Saint Denis. They are there today, interred with the rest of the Bourbons.

The drama of the French Revolution is as compelling today as it was when it took place, over two hundred years ago. Literature, art, poetry, and music have all undertaken to capture the spirit and the emotion of the age. Contrasted with its cousin, the American Revolution, it stands as a tragic reminder that not all rebellions—even those made in the name of democracy and freedom—succeed. Yet, the ideas and ideals that gave birth to those bloody years in France have lived on.

Throughout most of her life, Marie Antoinette was a pawn in the hands of others—her mother, her brothers, her husband, and finally the enraged people of France. A woman of little formal education, trained to be a pleasing and graceful ornament, Marie Antoinette gradually found her own strength. She was not destined to change the course of history, but to be a symbol of the old order that modern economic and social development was changing. Ironcially, even though she was not French herself, her role in the doomed monarchy of her adopted country, has made her a part of French history forever.

Glossary

l'Autrichienne French word for "Austrian woman," punning on the French word for female dog, *chienne*.

avocat A lawyer.

Bastille A French prison that stood as a symbol of oppression for many years. Bastille Day, July 14th, is the national holiday of France, commemorating the rise of the people against their oppressors.

berlin A carriage.

Bois de Boulogne A large wooded park on the edge of Paris.

Bourbon A ruling family of France from which Louis XVI was descended.

château A castle.

le coucher The evening undressing ritual, the opposite of the morning *lever*.

dauphin The eldest son of a king of France; the heir to the throne.

dauphine The wife of the dauphin.

fleur-de-lis The image of an iris in artistic design and heraldry, also the symbol of the French royal family.

gendarme A policeman.

hamlet A small village.

Hapsburg A powerful ruling family of Austria, from which

Marie Antoinette was descended.

le lever The morning ritual of rising and dressing. Initiated by Louis XIV, this public viewing caused consternation to Marie Antoinette because her private life was not really private.

Lorraine A region in northeastern France.

menagerie A place where animals, especially wild or foreign ones, are kept and trained.

naïve Unaffectedly simple; not possessing worldly wisdom.

Napoleon Emperor of France from 1804 to 1815.

orangerie A protected place; a greenhouse for raising oranges in cool climates.

proxy A marriage celebrated in the absence of the marriage bride or groom.

quartiers The neighborhoods of Paris.

queen consort The wife of a reigning king not crowned in her own right.

rendez-vous A meeting at an appointed time and place.

Rheims A city in northeastern France.

toilette The French word for getting dressed in the morning and undressed in the evening: washing, combing one's hair, etc.

tribunal A court of justice.

tricolor cockade A red, white, and blue ornament worn as a badge, usually pinned to the hat or the dress.

trousseau The clothes and accessories of a bride as well as other personal possessions.

Versailles A city and a palace outside of Paris where the French court resided.

voleuse French for a female thief.

Timeline

1755   The Archduchess Marie Antoinette is born in Vienna, Austria.

1765   Her father, Francis of Lorraine, dies.

1768   Negotiations for her marriage to the dauphin of France begin.

1770   Marries Louis Auguste of France, becoming the dauphine, at Versailles.

1773   Visits Paris for the first time.

1774   King Louis XV dies, leaving his heir, Louis Auguste, to rule France.

1775   Louis Auguste is crowned Louis XVI.

1778   Gives birth to her first child, Marie Thérèse Charlotte.

1780   Her mother, Empress Maria Theresa of Austria, dies.

1781   Marie Antoinette's first son, Louis Joseph Xavier, the dauphin, is born.

1785   Gives birth to her third child, Louis Charles, duc de Normandie; becomes entangled in the scandal of the Diamond Necklace Affair.

1786   Gives birth to her last child, Sophie Hélène Béatrice.

1787   Princess Sophie dies.

1789   The dauphin, Louis Joseph, dies; the French Revolution begins.

1791   Marie Antoinette escapes from the Tuileries Palace
        in Paris with her family; they are captured in
        Varennes, returned to Paris, and arrested.

1793   Louis XVI is executed by guillotine; Marie Antoin-
        ette is imprisoned in the Conciergerie, declared
        guilty of high treason, and sentenced to death by the
        guillotine. On October 16, she is executed.

Sources

CHAPTER ONE: An Archduchess is Born

p. 13, "My subjects are . . ." Annunziata Asquith, *Marie Antoinette* (New York: Taplinger Publishing Company, 1974), 16.

p. 14, "Gentlemen, why such gloomy faces?" Ibid.

p. 16, "Don't mind me . . ." Carolly Erickson, *To the Scaffold: The Life of Marie Antoinette* (New York: William Morrow and Company, Inc., 1991), 27.

p. 17, "They are born to obey . . ." Antonia Fraser, *Marie Antoinette: The Journey* (New York: Doubleday, 2001), 21.

p. 21, "Where is my Toinette . . ." Joan Haslip, *Marie Antoinette* (New York: Grove Press, 1988), 1.

p. 22, "God knows how much . . ." Ibid.

CHAPTER TWO: Preparing for Marriage

p. 31, "As for her French . . ." Haslip, *Marie Antoinette*, 5.

p. 33, "Farewell, my dearest child . . ." Fraser, *Marie Antoinette*, 53.

CHAPTER THREE: La Dauphine

p. 37, "Do not speak German, gentlemen; from today . . ." André Castelot, *Queen of France: A Biography of Marie*

Antoinette, trans. Denise Folliot (New York: Harper & Brothers, 1957), 20.

p. 37, "Our Archduchess in her debut at Strasbourg . . ." Dorothy Moulton Mayer, *Marie Antoinette: The Tragic Queen* (New York: Coward-McCann, Inc., 1968), 19.

p. 43, "not above twelve" Fraser, *Marie Antoinette*, 69.

CHAPTER FOUR: Everyday Life at Versailles

p. 51, "At eleven o'clock I have my hair done . . ." Ibid., 75.

p. 51, "in front of the whole world." Ibid., 76.

p. 52, "I hope that with . . ." Castelot, *Queen of France*, 44.

p. 54, "We wait for the King. . . ." Manuel and Odette Komroff, *Marie Antoinette* (New York: Julian Messner, 1967), 39.

p. 55, "I find my wife charming . . ." Castelot, *Queen of France*, 45.

p. 56, "I have made sure . . ." Vincent Cronin, *Louis and Antoinette* (New York: William Morrow & Company, Inc., 1975), 51.

p. 57, "riding spoils the complexion . . ." Komroff, *Marie Antoinette*, 40.

p. 65, "Madame . . . you have before you two hundred . . ." Komroff, *Marie Antoinette*, 46.

p. 65, "Oh God protect us, we . . ." Moulton Mayer, *Marie Antoinette*, 57.

CHAPTER FIVE: Too Young to Reign

p. 75, "The anointing was perfect . . ." Asquith, *Marie Antoinette*, 74.

p. 82, "My daughter is hastening to her ruin." Castelot, *Queen of France*, 148.

p. 83, "It is time—more than time—to reflect . . ." Fraser, *Marie Antoinette*, 155.

CHAPTER SIX: Royal Indulgences

p. 97, "The queen was received very coldly . . ." Castelot, *Queen of France,* 188.

p. 97, "What have I done to . . ." Ibid.

CHAPTER SEVEN: The Diamond Necklace Affair

p. 104, "You may hope . . ." Castelot, *Queen of France,* 208.

p. 106, "Who, then, was her . . ." Maxime de la Rocheterie, *The Life of Marie Antoinette,* vol. 1, trans. Cora Hamilton Bell (New York: Dodd, Mead and Company, 1893), 308.

p. 109, "The Queen's death . . ." Will and Ariel Durant, *The Story of Civilization Part X: Rousseau and Revolution* (New York: Simon and Schuster, 1967), 943.

CHAPTER EIGHT: The Beginning of the End

p. 115, "My elder son . . ." Fraser, *Marie Antoinette,* 260.

p. 116, "Death of my son . . ." Ibid., 276.

p. 120, "But this is a revolt . . ." Evelyne Lever, *Marie Antoinette: The Last Queen of France,* trans. Catherine Temerson, (New York: Farrar, Straus and Giroux, 2000), 212-213.

p. 120-1, "I know I missed the opportunity . . ." Ibid., 214.

p. 122, "Hang the Queen . . ." Erickson, *To the Scaffold,* 239.

p. 123, "We shall not need bread now . . ." Moulton Mayer, *Marie Antoinette,* 190.

p. 126, "Long live the Nation!" Fraser, *Marie Antoinette,* 345.

CHAPTER NINE: The Queen's Last Days

p. 143, "Vive la république . . ." Erickson, *To the Scaffold,* 345.

p. 144, "Monsieur, I ask . . ." Castelot, *Queen of France,* 409.

Bibliography

Asquith, Annunziata. *Marie Antoinette.* New York: Taplinger Publishing Company, 1974.

Belloc, Hilaire. *Marie Antoinette.* New York & London: G.P. Putnam's Sons, 1925.

Bernier, Olivier. *Louis XIV: A Royal Life.* New York: Doubleday, 1987.

Bernier, Olivier. *Secrets of Marie Antoinette.* Garden City, New York: Doubleday & Company, Inc., 1985.

Buranelli, Vincent. *Louis XIV.* New York: Twayne Publishers, Inc., 1966.

Castelot, André. *Queen of France: A Biography of Marie Antoinette.* Trans. Denise Folliot. New York: Harper & Brothers, 1957.

Cronin, Vincent. *Louis and Antoinette.* New York: William Morrow & Company, Inc., 1975.

De La Rocheterie, Maxime. *The Life of Marie Antoinette.* Vol. 1. Trans. Cora Hamilton Bell. New York: Dodd, Mead and Company, 1893.

Durant, Will, and Ariel Durant. *The Story of Civilization Part X: Rousseau and Revolution.* New York: Simon and Schuster, 1967.

Erickson, Carolly. *To the Scaffold: The Life of Marie Antoinette*. New York: William Morrow and Company, Inc., 1991.

Farr, Evelyn. *Marie Antoinette and Count Axel Fersen: The Untold Love Story*. London & Chester Springs, PA: Peter Owen Publishers, 1995.

Fraser, Antonia. *Marie Antoinette: The Journey*. New York: Doubleday, 2001.

Hardman, John. *Louis XVI*. New Haven & London: Yale University Press, 1993.

Haslip, Joan. *Marie Antoinette*. New York: Grove Press, 1988.

Komroff, Manuel and Komroff, Odette. *Marie Antoinette*. New York: Julian Messner, 1967.

Lever, Evelyne. *Marie Antoinette: The Last Queen of France*. Trans. Catherine Temerson. New York: Farrar, Straus and Giroux, 2000.

Mossiker, Frances. *The Queen's Necklace*. New York: Simon and Schuster, 1961.

Moulton Mayer, Dorothy. *Marie Antoinette: The Tragic Queen*. New York: Coward-McCann, Inc., 1968.

Seward, Desmond. *Marie Antoinette*. New York: St. Martin's Press, 1981.

Web sites

http://www.austrian-mint.com/e/mahitxt.html
A biography of the queen, hosted by the Austrian Mint.

http://www.chateauversailles.fr/
The official web site of Versailles.

http://www.distinguishedwomen.com/biographies/maria-th.html
A biography of Marie Antoinette's mother, Maria Theresa.

http://chnm.gmu.edu/revolution/
A comprehensive and informative siteabout the French Revolution, with a great number of illustrations.

http://www.ac.wwu.edu/~stephan/Rulers/bourbon.html
The Bourbon family tree.

Index